Trilogy of Treason

Trilogy of Treason
An Intertextual Study
of Juan Goytisolo

Michael Ugarte

University of Missouri Press
Columbia & London, 1982

Library of Congress Cataloging in Publication Data

Ugarte, Michael, 1949–
 Trilogy of Treason.

 Bibliography: p. 162
 1. Goytisolo, Juan—Criticism and interpretation. I. Title.
PQ6613.079Z97   863'.64   81–10288
ISBN 0–8262–0353–1   AACR2

To Mercedes and the
Pleasant Street McCarthys

A Note on the Translations

All translations of the trilogy are taken from the published English versions: *Marks of Identity*, translated by Gregory Rabassa (New York: Grove Press, 1969); *Count Julian*, translated by Helen R. Lane (New York: Viking, 1974); *Juan the Landless*, translated by Helen R. Lane (New York: Viking, 1977). All page numbers following the translations refer to these editions. Any other translations of Spanish or French are my own unless otherwise indicated. In most cases, the poetic qualities of the cited prose and poetry have been sacrificed for a clear rendering of the original. In translating the more difficult texts, however (Antonio Machado's "El mañana efímero," for example), I have expressed my own interpretations, which are (as are all interpretations) open to dialogue.

Preface

Of all contemporary peninsular novelists who have achieved recognition outside of Spain, one of the most important is Juan Goytisolo. His fame is largely due to the condition of his exile. Goytisolo has said on several occasions that had he not taken up residence outside Spain, he would never have written the novels that have made him an international figure: *Marks of Identity*, *Count Julian*, and *Juan the Landless*. An author's assessment of his own work is admittedly suspect, but Goytisolo's praise of exile does pinpoint an important element in his writing: his move to Paris allowed him to assimilate certain literary concepts that were not part of the intellectual climate of Spain. In my view, Goytisolo's apprehension of these concepts and his growing disaffection toward everything Spanish are the prime sources of his writing, and they are the subjects of this book.

Writers who reject their native lands and reside in other countries (James Joyce and Samuel Beckett are noteworthy examples) become exposed to new influences that drastically change their perception of the world and their writing. Goytisolo's role as reader, therefore, is at least as important as his role as writer. For this reason, my point of departure is an examination of intertextuality, a structuralist notion of the presence of texts within texts. The term *intertextuality*, which is employed by French theoreticians such as Roland Barthes and Julia Kristeva as well as by contemporary Latin American "boom" writers, is crucial to the whole of Goytisolo's undertaking—his attempt to corrupt, subvert, and thus betray the aesthetic and thematic concerns of other authors.

Because of the dearth of theoretical discussions of Goytisolo, certain critics have been led into taking an unquestioning stance in regard to the success or failure of Goytisolo's work. In my analysis I have attempted to distance my discourse from that of

Goytisolo. This posture has been difficult for me in the light of my personal feelings of repugnance for so many facets of Francisco Franco's Spain, a repugnance that, I admit, initially inspired my interest in Goytisolo. Yet through the perspective I have chosen, I have come to conclude that Goytisolo's assimilation of "foreign" notions of modern literary theory has been conditioned by his obsession with his own culture, a blind spot that makes his understanding of these ideas questionable and problematic.

My journey through Goytisolo's writing has led me to a variety of other texts. I remain disturbed by Goytisolo's misreading of these other texts at the same time as I marvel at the uniqueness of his interpretations. My reading of Goytisolo has affected my rereading of such diverse authors as Miguel de Cervantes, Mariano José de Larra, the figures of the Generation of '98, Octavio Paz, Américo Castro, and T. E. Lawrence. I wish to thank Goytisolo for a new perspective on these old texts and to beg his forgiveness for an occasional tone of disapproval.

I also want to thank the many people and organizations who played a part in the completion of this project. The two people to whom I owe utmost gratitude are John Kronik, the prime reader of the manuscript in its formative stage of development, and Maurita Ugarte McCarthy. Professor Kronik's insights into theoretical problems, especially in relation to a specific work of literature; his keen ability to pick out structural inconsistencies; his acute, at times frustrating, sensitivity to stylistic flaws are all felt on virtually every page of this book. No less an aid in the preparation of my work has been Maurita McCarthy. A judicious and diligent reader with a thorough grasp of literary problems, she made innumerable suggestions that I heeded scrupulously. In addition, our many dialogues on certain issues and problems raised in my analysis led to valuable improvements.

Further gratitude is due to those who read the manuscript, or parts of it, and offered encouraging and fruitful comments: David Grossvogel, Enrico Santí, Roberto González Echevarría, the late Bertel Pedersen, Beth Goldsmith, and Terry Rafferty, all presently or at one time at Cornell University. I should also like to thank Julian Palley for an encouraging reading.

A special note of thanks is due to the staff of the University of Missouri Press; to my typists, Sara Hedberg and Marsha Silvey; and to Wayne Hines for his aid in the preparation of the final manuscript.

I wish to express further gratitude to the editors of *Modern Fiction Studies* and *Journal of Spanish Studies: Twentieth Century* for allowing me to include parts of my articles in this book.

M. U.
Columbia, Mo.
8 May 1981

Contents

Trilogy of Treason

Introduction

Francisco Franco's Spain has produced a series of cultural achievements in spite of its oppressive political and social structure. Many Spanish writers and artists, however, have been alienated from their country spatially (by the necessity to reside elsewhere) and existentially (by their feeling of estrangement from their native land). Such expatriates of the Franco era as Max Aub, Rafael Alberti, Fernando Arrabal, and Luis Buñuel are representative of a breed of artists who have found their country's intellectual, social, and political climate stifling and prohibitive. Their only alternative has been to leave their homeland, to begin a new life in an alien society. In many cases, the condition of exile has created tensions that have set the tone and have ultimately defined these artists' work. Juan Goytisolo is an example: he is a renegade, a writer who seeks to rid himself of the culture that has shaped his existence.

The son of parents who supported Franco and who had profited from lucrative sugar plantations in colonial Cuba, Goytisolo acquired leftist political convictions at the University of Barcelona and broke with his past. In 1956, at the age of twenty-five, after a series of problems with censorship, police interrogations, and the detainments of his brother Luis, Goytisolo chose to live and write in France. Yet even though he renounced Spain, he returned on numerous occasions to document and reflect on his estranged homeland. Spain is perhaps the most crucial theme in Goytisolo's works, for it is the inspiration for the declamatory and aggressive nature of his novels.

Goytisolo's rebelliousness seems to intensify with every new novel that he writes from *Juegos de manos* (1954) to *Juan sin tierra* (1975). There was a break, however, in this intensification, a period in which he became unsatisfied with his past work and embarked on a new literary endeavor. This break is evidenced by a

1

dramatic change in his style and technique as well as by the onset of an all-out attack on Spanish culture. The weapon of that attack is not the realistic exposé of Spanish society that had character-ized the early novels (1954–1966) but verbal contamination, a linguistic venom that Goytisolo uses to destroy the Spanish language itself. Goytisolo's new concept of writing assumes that the foundations of "sacred Spain," his number-one enemy, are its texts, which, in addition to literature, include political, philo-sophical, and religious texts as well as nonlinguistic forms of communication, such as music, photography, and painting. For this reason, the main conflict in Goytisolo's later prose (1966 to the present) is a conflict between texts, an intertextual struggle among voices, codes, and diverse forms of writing. This new direction is the thrust of Goytisolo's trilogy of treason—*Señas de identidad (Marks of Identity)*, *Reivindicación del Conde don Julián (Count Julian)*, and *Juan sin tierra (Juan the Landless)*—which manifest a concept of writing as an intertextuality.[1] Although the attempt to subvert, corrupt, and contaminate the mother country through an intertextual process comes to the fore in this tripartite cycle, the seeds of this concept of writing are also evident in the early novels.

The Early Novels (1954–1966)

The publication of *Juegos de manos (Sleight of Hand)*, 1954, and *Duelo en el paraíso (Duel in Paradise)*, 1955,[2] established Goytisolo's reputation as one of Spain's most promising young novelists. These first two novels, however, have little in common with the innovation and linguistic experimentation of *Señas*, *Don Julián*, and *Juan sin tierra*. Both *Juegos* and *Duelo* are examples of a novelistic orientation that was predominant in the fifties. At that time there was a reaction against the vanguardist nuances of the pre-civil-war period, a movement whose leading theoretician was José Ortega y Gasset. After the civil war, writers such as Camilo José Cela, Carmen Laforet, and Ana María Matute attempted to depict Spanish life as realistically as possible while paying close attention to detail and to social problems. The trend toward social criticism continued with younger writers whose recollection of the war was not as immediate.[3] The literary experiments of the twenties and thirties (works by Ramón Pérez de Ayala, Benjamín Jarnés, and Ramón Gómez de la Serna) were seen by socially committed writers as frivolous and elitist games that manifested a blatant disregard for the social plight of the twentieth-century Spaniard. Goytisolo participated in the promulgation of these anti-Ortegian views not only in his practice of the novel (*Juegos, Duelo,* and virtually all his literary production prior to *Señas*) but also in essays and journalistic pieces that advanced social causes and socially committed literature. Firmly agreeing with Aub's assessment of post-civil-war literature, Goytisolo wrote, "Hay que humanizarse o perecer" ("humanize or perish").[4]

The type of social realism advanced by Goytisolo and by other writers of the fifties was not, however, a call for a return to the nineteenth-century historical novels of Benito Pérez Galdós and Clarín [Leopoldo Alas]. The term *realist* was defined in a different way. Galdós, Clarín, and other giants of nineteenth-century realism (Charles Dickens, Honoré de Balzac, Leo Tolstoy) portrayed society from an omniscient standpoint. They were on the outside looking in, and the angle of their novelistic lens allowed them to encompass everything: all life, all human interaction. The nineteenth-century historical novel was an attempt to make sense out of reality; the powerful social and historical forces were synthesized, laid bare, and clarified. In the Spain of the fifties, however, the novelistic portrayal of reality was not and could not be all-encompassing. Reality had become too complex and too irrational, and any attempt to order its components was futile. Reality was limited to what one could see, hear, touch, taste, and smell and was no longer guided by the same external and intangible forces that were at work in Galdós. In Cela's *Pascual Duarte* and *La colmena (The Beehive)* and in Goytisolo's *Juegos* and *Duelo,* there is an intense attention to detail, to objects, to what one can apprehend through the senses.[5]

At times, reality becomes so intricate, so indifferent to the misery and horror that it evidences, that the reader winces not only at the conditions pictured in the writing but also at the indifference with which these situations are described.

Juegos de manos is the story of a group of pampered, valueless, and disillusioned young men and women whose rebellion against the social order is fruitless and self-indulgent. This gang of self-appointed *enfants terribles* plans the assassination of a political official and tricks David, the most sensitive member of the group, into executing the plan. But David, who is too innocent to carry out the duty ascribed to him, falls prey to Agustín, the strongest and most cynical member of the bunch. The assassin becomes the victim precisely because of his tragic flaw—his distaste for violence. These adolescents are deeply troubled human beings, victims of the horrors of war who are unable to channel their hatred of the status quo into a meaningful opposition. Yet Goytisolo's sympathy for them is minimal. Throughout *Juegos* Goytisolo steadfastly refrains from commenting on the merit (or lack of it) of his characters' actions, on their relationships with their parents, on their pranks, on their childhood memories. Goytisolo's eye is that of a photographer, seemingly indifferent yet, in the last analysis, devastatingly critical.

Duelo en el paraíso takes a similar approach to the portrayal of Spanish life. The culprit in *Duelo*, however, is the civil war itself—death, destruction, and the disappearance of genuine human affection. Goytisolo's ironic "paradise" is in reality a hell: bombs explode constantly, multitudes of people die, individuals suffer physical and psychological wounds, children play war games that ultimately cause the death of a sympathetic character, Abel (reminiscent of David in *Juegos*). We witness all this chaos through the experiences of Martín Elósegui who, as a result of the war, loses everything that made his life meaningful: his lover and the child she was about to bear. Again the reality that Goytisolo has chosen to describe is less than pleasant, but he never tells us so. In the following passage he describes the atmosphere in which the displaced refugee children must live.

La carretera dejaba a sus orillas un reguero de muerte: soldados ametrallados por los aviones, presos fusilados al borde del camino, desertores con una bala en la nuca. Los niños se movían entre ellos como peces en el agua, dando gritos y órdenes guturales, absorbiendo los modos de los mayores, vistiéndose con los despojos de los muertos y acumulando en sus escondrijos los frutos de su juego. También la guerra sembraba en su cortejo algunas flores: los chiquillos que robaban el camión de la Intendencia, jugaban a la nieve con los sacos de azúcar; el gorro de un coronel, salpicado aún de sangre, cubría inmediatamente el cráneo del cabecilla. Los niños aspiraban a las condecoraciones más elevadas. Pasaban de contra-bando a través de las líneas de combate, se adornaban con banderas de uno y otro ejército. Diminutos Gulliveres en el país de los gigantes, aprendían el mecanismo de las granadas, y mataban a los pájaros con cargas de dinamita. (p. 21)

(The road left a furrow of death on each side: soldiers machine-gunned by fighter planes, executed prisoners, deserters with a bullet in their necks. The children moved about them like fish in water, shouting orders, screaming, absorbing the ways of their elders, wearing the dead men's military garb, and storing the booty in their hiding places.
The war also sowed a few flowers in the wake of its funeral train: the gang of children who stole the charnel wagon played with sacks of sugar pretending they were in a snowstorm; a colonel's hat, still spotted with blood, immediately covered the gang leader's head. The children aspired to receiving the highest military decorations. They crossed the lines of combat like contraband; they adorned themselves with flags of various armies. Miniature Gullivers in the land of giants, they learned how to set off grenades and killed birds with dynamite.)

Of note in this description is the narrator's seeming disregard for the nature of what he describes. The elements of the scene are accumulated one after the other as if the narrator were making a list: "machine-gunned soldiers," "executed prisoners," "desert-ers," and in the next paragraph, "sacks of sugar" and "a colonel's hat." The children's games among the corpses, their absorption and imitation of the bellicose behavior of their elders, and their killing of birds with dynamite do not appear to be of any consequence to the narrator. Reality is allowed to speak for itself.

This passage, which is typical of Goytisolo's early writing, might lead critics to characterize him as a *tremendista*, as does Kessel Schwartz.[6] Yet *tremendismo*, the depiction of the most outlandish, repulsive, and gory situations in order to evoke the misery and deprivation of Spanish life after the civil war, is not Goytisolo's intent. His early preoccupation is not to shock but to capture certain aspects of reality and to allow readers to react as they see fit. Goytisolo's early novels are better described as neorealistic, artistic reproductions of tangible reality that are characterized by an emphasis on sensorial phenomena and by a minimum of explanation of that reality's significance. Any conclusions, as unpleasant as they may be, are left to the reader.

In 1956, the year of his departure from the Iberian peninsula, Goytisolo embarked on a new literary adventure that was still very much in tune with the neorealism of his first two novels but was characterized by the appearance of a new technique. He conceived of a series of three novels based on a poem by Antonio Machado, "El mañana efímero" ("The Ephemeral Future"), and titled it *El pasado efímero (The Ephermeral Past): Fiestas, El circo (The Circus), La resaca (The Undertow).*[7] Goytisolo's use of Machado's poetic assessment of the Spain of yesterday, today, and tomorrow signals the beginning of his conscious employment of themes from other texts as well as his radical reassessment of Spanish culture. By making Machado his model, Goytisolo opens his social criticism to another written world. Placing *El pasado efímero* (which is the title of another Machado poem) in a textual relationship with another work broadens the thematic framework and allows the introduction of other elements with which Goytisolo can carry on a dialogue, a dialogue that eventually becomes an open war.

Each volume of *El pasado efímero* begins with a segment from Machado's forty-two-line poem that evokes the future of Spain through a depiction of the past. Epigraphs are hardly uncommon in literature, yet in Goytisolo's three novels Machado's poem assumes a function that transcends the mere inscription of an idea or image from another text. Examining the relationship between *El pasado efímero* and "El mañana efímero," one finds that the poem governs the themes and structures of the novels. Although Goytisolo chose fragments that were most directly suited to his own work, the presence of Machado's poem is felt in its entirety.[8]

El Mañana Efímero

La España de charanga y pandereta,
cerrado y sacristía,
devota de Frascuelo y de María,
de espíritu burlón y de alma quieta,
ha de tener su mármol y su día,   5
su infalible mañana y su poeta.
El vano ayer engendrará un mañana
vacío y ¡por ventura! pasajero.
Será un joven lechuzo y tarambana,
un sayón con hechuras de bolero,   10
a la moda de Francia realista,
un poco al uso de París pagano,
y al estilo de España especialista
en el vicio al alcance de la mano.
Esa España inferior que ora y bosteza,   15
vieja y tahúr, zaragatera y triste;
esa España inferior que ora y embiste,
cuando se digna usar de la cabeza,
aún tendrá luengo parto de varones
amantes de sagradas tradiciones   20
y de sagradas formas y maneras;
florecerán las barbas apostólicas,
y otras calvas en otras calaveras
brillarán, venerables y católicas.
El vano ayer engendrará un mañana   25
vacío y ¡por ventura! pasajero,
la sombra de un lechuzo tarambana,
de un sayón con hechuras de bolero:
el vacuo ayer dará un mañana huero.
Como la náusea de un borracho ahíto   30
de vino malo, un rojo sol corona
de heces turbias las cumbres de granito;
hay un mañana estomagante escrito
en la tarde pragmática y dulzona.
Mas otra España nace,   35
la España del cincel y de la maza,
con esa eterna juventud que se hace
del pasado macizo de la raza.
Una España implacable y redentora,
España que alborea   40
con un hacha en la mano vengadora,
España de la rabia y de la idea.

(The Ephemeral Future)

(The Spain of brass band and tambourine,

and sacristy, closed
and devoted to Francis and Mary,
a mocking spirit and quiet soul,
will have its marble and its day,   5
its infallible tomorrow and its poet.
Yesterday will spawn in its vanity,
an empty and, perchance, fleeting new day.
It will be a young and mulish crackpot,
an executioner in the guise of a bolero dancer,   10
in the mode of royalist France,
a bit as in pagan Paris,
and in the style of a Spain
specialized in freely accessible vice.
That inferior Spain which prays and yawns,   15
old and deceitful, boisterous and sad;
that inferior Spain which prays and attacks,
when the time calls for the mind,
will still bear, after a long labor,
men who love sacred traditions   20
and sacred ways and forms;
apostolic beards will flourish,
and the bald spots will shine
on new venerable and Catholic skulls.
Yesterday will spawn in its vanity,   25
an empty and, perchance, fleeting tomorrow,
the shadow of a mulish crackpot,
of an executioner in the guise of a bolero dancer:
a vacuous yesterday will give way to an empty tomorrow.
Like the vomit of a drunkard sick   30
from bad wine, a red sun crowns
the granite peaks with dregs;
there is a tomorrow written with an aching stomach
in the pragmatic and sickeningly sweet afternoon.
But another Spain is born,   35
the Spain of the hammer and chisel,
with that eternal youth made from
the solid past of the race.
A Spain implacable and redemptive,
a Spain that dawns   40
with an ax in its vengeful hand,
Spain of rage and ideas.)

In "El mañana efímero," there is a shift from the description of the Spanish past (lines 1–34) to the expression of a vision of the future (lines 35–42). In Goytisolo's trilogy, *Fiestas* and *El circo* reflect the first section of the poem, and *La resaca* reflects the second. There is an underlying irony throughout Machado's text in his use of the future tense ("España . . . aún tendrá") to evoke the past and in the use of the present tense to convey the future. In Goytisolo, there is no interplay between verb tenses, yet in all three novels, the history of Spain unfolds through the depiction of present-day characters and situations that resemble figures and events of the past.

The three novels of *El pasado efímero* take place during a religious holiday that creates a festive atmosphere and shapes the narrative. Similarly, Machado's poem begins

La España de charanga y pandereta,
cerrado y sacristía,
devota de Frascuelo y de María,
de espíritu burlón y de alma quieta,
ha de tener su mármol y su día.

The brass band and the tambourine, as well as the religious figures "Frascuelo" and "María," evoke a sense of festivity in the poem that is akin to the atmosphere in Goytisolo's novels. In *Fiestas*, there is a contrast between the religious congress that organizes the celebration and the *murcianos* who live in shacks on the outskirts of the town. (A *murciano* is a person from Murcia, but Goytisolo's characters apply the word to all poor people from the south of Spain.) As the congress prepares for the holidays, the plight of the squatters intensifies until they are finally dispossessed from their dwellings at the height of the celebration. "El mañana efímero" contains a similar criticism of the church in the contrast between the gaiety and happiness of a religious holiday (the band and the tambourine) and the "espíritu burlón," the mocking spirit that, later in the poem, engenders the executioner in the guise of a bolero dancer. This image appears throughout the poem in the repetition of the tenth line, "un sayón con hechuras de bolero" (see line 28), and in the grotesque images: "borracho ahíto," "un lechuzo tarambana," "un rojo sol corona / de heces turbias las cumbres de granito." Not only is the festivity of this brass band destroyed; its reasons for being, the "barbas apostólicas" and the "calvas católicas," crumble with it. In *Fiestas* Goytisolo similarly creates an opposing relationship through two visions of Spain, that of the religious congress and that of the *murcianos*. Goytisolo counterposes the two realities of Spanish life as does Machado ("España que ora y bosteza" [line 15]). The specific fragment of the Machado poem inscribed in *Fiestas* (lines 17–21) is marked by a dominant image of religious fanaticism.

> Esa España inferior que ora y embiste,
> cuando se digna usar de la cabeza,
> aún tendrá luengo parto de varones
> amantes de sagradas tradiciones
> y de sagradas formas y maneras.

A Spain that prays and charges like a bull ("embiste, / cuando se digna usar de la cabeza") alludes not only to the sacred and bellicose traditions of the past but to the endurance of these traditions as they become the "formas y maneras" of the present. This thematic direction is exactly the same as that taken by Goytisolo in *Fiestas*. In the final chapter of the work, the main characters, whose lives had previously been indirectly connected, appear together during the commencement of the religious procession. Pipo, who has lost his innocence through his relationship with "Gorila," decides to march in the procession, against the advice of Professor Ortega, who has lost his job for refusing to participate in the festivities. Goytisolo describes the defeated expression on the professor's face when Pipo, the only one who had listened to this man of letters, bids him farewell for the last time. Don Paco beckons Pipo to continue along his way. He says (p. 221): "Anda, ven. No le hagas caso. Es un pobre fracasado. Un resentido social" ("Come along. Don't pay any attention to him. He's a failure. A social malcontent"). As the novel ends, the detailed description of the gala event (the

multitude of spectators, the colors of the religious vestments, the flowers thrown onto the street) is interrupted by a voice over the loudspeaker announcing the procession's arrival at its point of termination (pp. 222–23):

> *"El legado ha subido al trono de oro y púrpura e imparte la bendición al pueblo. . . . Todo el mundo llora, señores y señoras. . . . Imposible contener, ante tal explosión de fervor, la vista de las lágrimas."*

> *("The pope's emissary has stepped up to the golden throne and blesses the people. . . . Everyone is crying, ladies and gentlemen. . . . It's impossible to hold the tears in view of this explosive fervor.")*

and further on,

> *"Su ilustrísima bendice a los peregrinos desde su trono. . . . Las madres le tienden sus criaturas. . . . Todo el mundo, señores y señoras, intenta besar su manto."*

> *("His eminence blesses the pilgrims from his throne. . . . Mothers give him their infants to be blessed. . . . Everyone, ladies and gentlemen, is trying to kiss his garment.")*

The Spain that charges, yawns, and prays appears through the words of this loudspeaker, which assures its listeners of the righteousness and glory of the church and the Spanish nation.

The second novel in this trilogy, *El circo*, continues in the festive vein of *Fiestas*. *El circo* takes place in the town of Las Caldas, whose inhabitants are celebrating the feast of San Saturnino, their patron saint. The fragment of Machado's poem used for this text (lines 7–10) concerns the future product of an empty Spanish past.

> El vano ayer engendrará un mañana
> vacío y ¡por ventura! pasajero.
> Será un joven lechuzo y tarambana,
> un sayón con hechuras de bolero.

Goytisolo renders this poetic depiction of Spanish society concrete through the creation of Utah, a character who embodies all the traits of the "tarambana" ("crackpot"). Utah is in many ways a clown, a bohemian who wastes his money and spends his life hiding behind masks. He constantly confuses his world of thoughts and dreams with reality. His only positive feature is his ability to make people laugh, but even this gift is a mixed blessing, for his antics are contagious: they have the power to bring his followers into his own distorted and confused world. Utah believes himself to be a dangerous assassin and warns his wife of the arrival in Las Caldas of a murderer—himself. Unable to extract reality from his dream world, he claims responsibility for a murder that he did not commit. Utah is not only a parasite and a crackpot; he is an executioner. Although he does not commit the crime, he is the embodiment of a dying Spain that persists in living in an archaic fantasy world of past grandeur. The thematic relationship between Goytisolo's novel and Machado's poem is clear. With the creation of Utah as a symbol of Spanish decadence, Goytisolo has rendered Machado's "joven lechuzo" into a real human being. He has brought the spirit of the poem to life.

The last segment of the three-part cycle of *El pasado efímero* is *La resaca*, in which the final eight lines of "El mañana efímero" appear, not at the beginning of the text but at the end.

> Mas otra España nace,
> la España del cincel y de la maza,
> con esa eterna juventud que se hace
> del pasado macizo de la raza.
> Una España implacable y redentora,
> España que alborea
> con un hacha en la mano vengadora,
> España de la rabia y de la idea.

Of the three novels in the trilogy, *La resaca* is by far the most ambiguous and complex in terms of its themes and in its relationship to Machado's poem. The final lines of the poem vary from the previous ones in their depiction of a potential for a bright Spanish future. Machado's synthesis of "la rabia" and "la idea" is in effect the unity that he desires for Spain. The use of the present tense ("España nace," "España alborea") to convey a more positive view of the future suggests that this longed-for synthesis is in fact becoming a reality.

In Goytisolo this positive element is missing. Instead we find a situation remarkably similar to that of *Fiestas*, in which the celebration of a religious holiday culminates in empty speeches full of praise for the great social accomplishments of the church and the regime. In *La resaca*, however, the relatively brief presence of Carlitos, a character similar to Pipo, is incongruous with *Fiestas*. While Pipo cynically participates in the religious celebration even after Professor Ortega makes him aware of the church's dishonesty and oppression, Carlitos refuses to do so. Since Carlitos's father was once a staunch defender of the church, the boy is chosen to deliver a speech welcoming the church delegate. But all he can bring himself to say is, " 'Delegado. . . Somos pobres. . . Mi padre. . .' " (p. 184). These desperate words are cut off by the loudspeaker, which continues in the same vein as the one in *Fiestas* (p. 184): " *'Un pueblo que es capaz de estas hazañas del espíritu, de estos encuentros con Dios, es un pueblo de seres fabulosos . . . puestos en el carril de la cultura' "* (" *'A nation that is capable of these spiritual accomplishments, of these encounters with God, is a nation of fabulous beings . . . beings [who are] placed on the path of culture' "*). Thus Carlitos's final speech fades into silence. The people listen indifferently to the omnipresent loudspeaker as the flags wave amid the happy and monotonous rhythm of the band (p. 185). The transformation in Machado between the "vano ayer" and another, brighter Spain that is being born is reflected in Goytisolo's transition from *Fiestas* to *La resaca*, from Pipo to Carlitos, from those who beg to kiss the cardinal's robes to those who gaze indifferently at the Spanish flag as the loudspeaker praises the wondrous accomplishments of postwar Spanish society. Yet Machado's ultimate transformation is unlike Goytisolo's ambiguous ending. The reader cannot be certain of what will emerge from Carlitos's unwillingness to accept the view of Spain handed to him by the clerics—indifference, defeat, further victimization, or a new struggle for freedom?

The last eight lines of Machado's poem also reveal a tension of which Goytisolo seems well aware. The archaic and grotesque image of Spain up to these final lines is incongruous with the sturdiness and youthful energy of the future that Machado evokes. In order for this bright new future to take shape, Spain must preserve some of those qualities that Machado ridicules in the first lines of the poem. The "eterna juventud" is made out of the "pasado macizo de la raza." One must ask how this promising future will take place if Spain remains unwilling to undergo a thorough process of change. Goytisolo's creation of concrete situations reveals how he has been disturbed by Machado's image: Goytisolo is uncertain that this Spanish past should be preserved at all; the perpetuation of the race evoked in "El mañana efímero" is of questionable value in *El pasado efímero*, as the change of title suggests. Goytisolo ends his first trilogy with this question unresolved, and he does not reopen the issue again until 1969 when he writes *Don Julián*.

In addition to the citation of a specific text as in *El pasado efímero*, there is another device in his early works: the use of characters whose function depends on the reader's recognition of an outside text. In these cases, the previous or outside text becomes a literary or historical figure whose name alone is suggestive of a series of texts or of a system of thought. One such instance revolves around a character who is reminiscent of Francisco Giner de los Ríos. This man appears not only in *El pasado efímero* but also in *Juegos de manos* as Agustín's father, the patient, liberal intellectual who actively pursues social justice. Similar characters reappear in Goytisolo's early novels, but the concrete relationship between the fictional character and the historical figure does not take form until *La resaca*, when Goytisolo names his character Giner. A trace of Agustín's father reappears in *Fiestas* as Professor Ortega,[9] whose struggle against the regime causes him to lose his teaching position. Although the connection is not clear at this point, the professor too is reminiscent of Giner de los Ríos, whose adherence to the liberal, activist social philosophy of Krausism forced him into exile from Madrid to Cádiz one year after the Bourbon restoration of 1874. One of the central aspects of Giner de los Ríos's social program was the concentration on an autonomous educational system free from the control of the church or the state. In his essays he frequently affirmed the necessity to educate all members of society, especially workers.[10] The ideology of Giner de los Ríos is put forth clearly in *La resaca* by Giner, a character who similarly loses his position because of his liberal convictions. His function in the novel is to offer a means of struggling against social and political subjugation. Giner is always dealing directly with workers and social outcasts in Mano's tavern. His wife and children do not understand his humanistic concerns and feel that he is the cause of their own disgraceful condition. At one point, he leads a newly formed committee whose purpose is to raise the social consciousness of the neighborhood dwellers and to build a union. Giner's social theory is unveiled as he attempts to find words that his listeners will understand. He tells them that the established order has robbed them not only of the materials necessary for subsistence (food, shelter, and so on) but also of the capacity to express those needs through language.

> Giner se enjugó el sudor de la frente. Lo que quería decir le parecía absolutamente claro pero, al traducirlo en palabras, la claridad se desvanecía. El mismo se daba cuenta de que su discurso era confuso y no hallaba la manera de evitarlo.
> Los hombres del Centro, explicó, se habían apropiado el lenguaje de los hombres de las Afueras. Antes las palabras eran como monedas: Pan, Justicia, Hombre, habían perdido su significado. (p. 148)

> (Giner brushed the sweat from his brow. What he wanted to say seemed perfectly clear, but when he put it into words the clarity disappeared. He was well aware that his speech was confusing, and he could not avoid it.
> The people in the center of town [the officials] had appropriated the language of the people [those who lived in the outskirts]. Before, these words were like coins: Bread, Justice, Man, had lost their meaning.)

The rallying cry of Giner de los Ríos—"Bread, Justice, Man"—loses its signification as these words are mouthed by the agents of "official Spain." The concept that Giner (the character) is trying to express becomes a reality as the radio drowns out the words of his speech (p. 148): "Por la radio, la Voz proseguía: '*Vosotros implantaréis el reino de la paz porque sois nobles*' " ("The voice over the radio continued: *'You shall establish a kingdom of peace, for you are noble'* "). [11] In this scene there is a textual exchange between Goytisolo and Giner de los Ríos (who is himself transformed into a text), as well as a hostile confrontation between the language of Giner and that of the radio, the official voice of the regime. In *La resaca* Goytisolo begins the process of a conscious dialogue among a variety of political positions and philosophical concepts.

During the period between the completion of *El pasado efímero* and the beginning of *Señas*, Goytisolo altered his writing style, and his rebellious feelings toward Spain and society became stronger. Goytisolo's attempt at pure objectivity culminated in a new series of texts: *Campos de Níjar (Land of Níjar)*, 1960; *La isla (The Island)*, 1961; *La Chanca*, 1962; and *Pueblo en marcha (People on the March)*, 1963.[12] Assuming the role of a social scientist, Goytisolo traveled to the area on which he was to write, researched his subject, and documented his findings. In this new phase, Goytisolo situated his discourse within a fictional framework *(La isla)* or among lyrical descriptions of the Spanish countryside *(Campos, La Chanca,* and *Pueblo)*. These works are examples of Goytisolo's travelogues, a subgenre of the novel re-created after the civil war by Cela in his *Viaje a la Alcarria (Trip to Alcarria)*. During this period of literary growth (1959–1963), Goytisolo felt an increasing need to confront the political reality of his country and to do everything he could as a novelist to change that reality. The travelogues were his primary weapons in that struggle for social change.

In the travelogues the dialogue between texts is no less important to the thematic structure than it was in *El pasado efímero*. Yet Goytisolo's manipulation of outside texts changes in the later group of works both through the types of outside texts that he selects and in the concept of writing implied by his use of this technique. In *Campos de Níjar*, which is a first-person account of a trip to Almería, Goytisolo depicts the misery and deplorable conditions of the people who lived in that backward province of Andalucía. Throughout the narrator's travels, we witness the sparse landscape, billboards, and advertisements, and we listen to the dialect spoken in the towns. At one point (p. 21), Goytisolo evokes the beauty of the countryside and, at the same time, condemns the oppression of the social order in a mixture of lyrical description and crass objectivity.

> Yo observo que la carretera está en buen estado, allanada, con su chispo de peralte en las curvas. . . . en los muros de las casuchas en ruinas, se repiten las inscripciones en pintura y alquitrán que me acompañan desde Almería,
> FRANCO
> FRANCO
> FRANCO

> (I observe that the road is in good condition, smooth and high at the curves. . . . on the walls that are left of the ruined roadside structures, the painted inscriptions appear over and over again accompanying me all the way from Almería,
> FRANCO
> FRANCO
> FRANCO)

Like *Campos, Pueblo en marcha* is a first-person account of a trip, this time to Cuba after the 1959 revolution. Although *Pueblo* is laudatory of a society, while *Campos* is harshly critical, the style and structure of both works are similar, if not identical. In both *Campos* and *Pueblo*, the outside texts are unlike those used in *El pasado efímero*. While that trilogy reminds the reader of other literary texts such as Machado's poem or Giner de los Ríos's essays and speeches, the outside texts contained in the travelogues are far more concrete. For example, as the narrator of *Pueblo* travels from one end of Cuba to the other recording what he sees, there are instances in which the words of a road sign or a slogan are transcribed into the text. Throughout the travelogues the outside texts are specific features of a social order, such as advertisements, popular songs, and proverbs. Spanish society is not exposed through a poetic re-creation of conventions and themes from literature, as is the case in *El pasado efímero,* but through the incorporation of unaltered bits and pieces of a culture.

In *La Chanca,* a deceptively simple work, segments of historical documents, other travelogues, and journalistic texts are collected in the form of appendixes. The use of these outside texts is appropriate to Goytisolo's objectivist technique, for they appear verbatim. Before these appendixes, Goytisolo relates a story of a Spaniard living in Paris who visits his homeland. As he travels to the city of Almería, the reader is confronted with a first-person description of the misery, hardship, and lack of freedom that the inhabitants of the poverty-stricken section of La Chanca must endure. The appendixes include a variety of documents from twelfth-century Arab accounts of the city to articles in contemporary Spanish periodicals such as *Incunable* and *Pueblo*. Through the inclusion of these texts, Goytisolo shows the chronological development of the city against the background of Spanish history. According to Mahamed-Al-Adrisi, the Arab commentator, Almería was a thriving commercial and industrial center characterized by the abundance of beautiful gardens. But with the reconquest, the commercial importance of Almería diminished. Through the subsequent renditions of trips to Almería by Spaniards and foreigners, the slow decline of the city becomes apparent as it is transformed into one of the most economically depressed regions in Spain.

La Chanca, one of Goytisolo's least-known works, marks the beginning of a concept of intertextuality that is brought to further fruition in *Señas*. It is the first hint of a linguistic attack on "la España oficial," an attempt to mesh the social criticism of the regime with a critique of that regime's language. In the appendixes of *La Chanca,* Goytisolo converts Spanish history into a series of texts, and in so doing, he undermines some of the accepted notions of the history of the peninsula. After descriptions of the squalor in which the people of La Chanca must live and after renditions of the atrocities committed by the Christians upon the Moors, we read (pp. 179–83) the official description of Almería that is promoted by the Ministry of Information and Tourism:

> La Chanca, *El más pintoresco barrio del mundo.* —Me gusta La Chanca. . . . La Chanca es un prodigio. . . . La Chanca nunca tiene las puertas

cerradas. Es ésta una gente hospitalaria, marinera, salobre, salitrosa . . . —A los pescadores . . . les resultaba muy cómodo vivir aquí . . . La Chanca está espléndida, en su alto pedestal.

(La Chanca, *The most picturesque place in the world.* —I like La Chanca. . . . La Chanca is a blessing. . . . La Chanca never closes its doors on anyone. Its seafaring people are hospitable, gracious, and kind . . . —It was quite advantageous for the fishermen to live here . . . La Chanca, on its pedestal, is splendid.)

When considered in conjunction with Goytisolo's eyewitness account of this section of Almería, the portrayals in the appendixes no longer seem objective renditions of situations and events. Because of the context in which they are situated, their signification has changed. Behind the voices of the writers of the official descriptions of La Chanca is the ironic authorial voice of Goytisolo. The two voices clash as Goytisolo loses all hints of objectivity and struggles to destroy the validity or "truth" of these documents. The word *objectivism* is, in the last analysis, a misnomer, for not only are Goytisolo's travelogues written from the point of view of one individual, a *yo,* but their existence in literature is the result of an ideological posture.

The Break with Realism

Examining the chronology of Goytisolo's literary production from 1954 to 1963, one notices the regularity with which he wrote: about one work each year beginning with *Juegos de manos* and ending with *La Chanca.* The first edition of his next full-length work of fiction, *Señas de identidad,* however, did not reach a printer until 1966. *Señas* evidenced a radical shift in Goytisolo's writing, although Schwartz continues to assert that the essential form and content of Goytisolo's novels have not changed significantly from *Juegos* to *Juan sin tierra.* After the publication of *Don Julián,* Schwartz wrote: "A careful reading of Goytisolo's latest novel . . . reveals that Goytisolo has not changed the essential elements of his pessimistic social vision, his preoccupation with Spanish culture, or his style. . . . In his latest novel, a summation and epitome of earlier ones, he merely intensifies, elaborates, and refines already existing elements." In his assessment of *Juan sin tierra,* Schwartz submitted that Goytisolo was repeating the personal and social constants of his previous novels.[13] Yet the differences between Goytisolo's early works and those published after 1963 are evident at first glance. Stylistically the early works are dominated by a linear narration chronologically ordered so that the reader has little difficulty in grasping the plot. The three days that transpire in *Señas de identidad,* on the other hand, are by no means as clearly delineated. They are interspersed with flashbacks that take us back before the civil war, through the war, to the present. Furthermore, the multiplicity of settings in *Señas* (Paris, diverse parts of Spain, Cuba) makes the reader's understanding of where the action is taking place no less problematic.[14] In *Don Julián* and in *Juan sin tierra* Goytisolo moves from chronological to mythical time, a technique that has the effect of synthesizing the past and future into an all-encompassing present. The trajectory of the second trilogy takes the reader to a variety of places and through a myriad of historical moments. Schwartz's argument, which is based more on content than on form, assumes that Goytisolo has always been engaged in the criticism of Spanish society and culture and that, in the latest novels, he "merely intensifies" what he has been doing all along. However, if one compares the early works with the most recent in the light of modern literary theory, one discovers that Goytisolo is indeed engaged in something new. Social criticism, the thrust of his earlier writing, implies the possibility of a change in society and thereby a change in the real life of human beings. This type of criticism is historical in nature and usually assumes the necessity of progress outside of literature, that is, in the realm of politics and society. In 1963 and 1964, Goytisolo looked back to his own literary production and viewed the notion of social criticism that it embodied as too narrow.[15] He wished to attack the object of his former criticism, sacred Spain, head-on. The act of writing was no longer a means to an end but had become an end in itself. Writing for Goytisolo was transformed into an act of liberation, an act of revolution, an assault, a destructive force that created new forms of thought and life.[16]

Goytisolo's move to Paris triggered that new direction in his writing and expanded his literary horizons to include non-Hispanic writers and texts: the discussion of Alain Robbe-Grillet in *Problemas de la novela (Problems in the Novel)* (pp. 63–70) is an example. Similarly, Goytisolo began to assimilate European structuralism not only as an aid in his understanding of literature but also as a tool in his destructive enterprise. One of the most important implements of destruction, the one that is at the core of his new concept of writing, is intertextuality. In the early novels we see hints of this concept (the voice of the radio in *Fiestas* and *La resaca,* the appendixes of *La Chanca*), but the intertextual conflict does not explode until Alvaro Mendiola sets out to discover his "signs of identity."

1. Juan Goytisolo's Theoretical Milieu

Juan Goytisolo tells us in his "Cronología" that his first trip to Paris in 1953 coincided with his first use of marijuana and with his ultimate confirmation that the underworld—the world of the lumpenproletariat, prostitutes, pimps, and drug pushers—was far more interesting than the insipid monotony of the bourgeoisie.[1] At the age of twenty-two, Goytisolo had already revealed his distaste for the conventional and, more important, for the sterility of Spanish society under Franco's regime. What he had not found, however, was the proper voice with which to lash out at the objects of his discontent. At that early stage, he was seeking a novelistic framework with which to set his rebelliousness into motion. By his own admission, the novels that he wrote prior to *Señas de identidad* were the products of a writer in search of a voice.[2]

In addition to marking a conclusive separation from the home of his parents and countrymen, Goytisolo's permanent move to Paris in 1956 furthered his career. Having lived at the mercy of the absurd condemnations of Spanish censorship, he found it financially and artistically beneficial to work for the Gallimard Publishing Company and to be able to write whatever he wanted. Paris, his new haven, as it was for so many Spanish exiles, was also the city of the avant-garde, the home of Jean-Paul Sartre, Jean Genet, Alain Robbe-Grillet, and Roland Barthes who in the fifties was laying the groundwork for his *Le degré zéro de l'écriture (Writing Degree Zero)* and *Essais critiques (Critical Essays)*. Sartre, Genet, Robbe-Grillet, and Barthes all entered Goytisolo's literary world, and some of them, as Genet did, even became his intimate friends. In Goytisolo's later essays, especially those compiled under the title *Disidencias (Dissidences)*, he laments the xenophobic character of the history of the Iberian peninsula, which he sees as the source of the typically Spanish cultural lag that he is trying to remedy. From *Problemas de la novela* through *El furgón de cola (The Caboose)* to *Disidencias,* one detects the cosmopolitan tone with which Goytisolo analyzes the strengths and shortcomings of his native land.[3] *Problemas* covers Italian, American, and French literature and makes interesting (while not very profound) observations on György Lukács, Bertolt Brecht, André Malraux, Natalie Sarraute, and many other non-Hispanic writers. *El furgón de cola* constantly compares the literature of Spain to that of other European countries, and *Disidencias* contains many references to structuralist and poststructuralist theoreticians. At first glance, it appears that Goytisolo wishes to establish himself as the preeminent assimilator of European (non-Hispanic) culture and to make that culture accessible to the Spanish reading public. While Goytisolo would probably deny it, there is some truth to this assessment. The cosmopolitan Goytisolo, who was familiar with diverse literary movements and theories, enjoyed the international reputation bestowed on him by the three volumes of his later trilogy. It is no less true that his assimilation of non-Hispanic culture, whether French, Afro-Cuban, or Arab, had a tremendous impact on his writing.

The structuralist movement, or activity, as Barthes called it in *Le degré zéro de l'écriture,* is an important new mode of thought that became popular in Paris during the late fifties, sixties, and seventies. Structuralism's influence on Goytisolo seems more evident with each volume of the trilogy, but Goytisolo's acceptance of certain tenets of structuralism by no means involves a total commitment to that mode of thought, nor does the exiled Spaniard ever declare himself a practicing structuralist. Rather than clinging religiously to any single viewpoint, Goytisolo in the Paris of the sixties and seventies blends various doctrines and points of view into a personal literary ideology. In his writing Goytisolo acts out the dialogue and subsequent conflict between existentialism and structuralism, as seen, for example, in Barthes's response to Sartre's *Qu'est-ce que la littérature (What Is Literature)* in *Le degré zéro,* both of which have Marxist overtones.[4] Goytisolo's fondness for certain concepts of the structuralist school, especially that of intertextuality, is at odds with one of the most salient features of his writing: the personal search for cultural (political, religious, sexual, and literary) authenticity. For an understanding of the tensions and complexities of his later works, it is essential to consider the impact of structuralism on Goytisolo and its at times unholy alliance with other literary trends.

What did this Spanish man of the world find so attractive about structuralism? What does the intertextual conflict of the trilogy have to do with contemporary literary theory in France? Most important, how does the concept of intertextuality develop from formalism to structuralism? Answers to the first two questions depend on a detailed response to the third, for, as we shall see, Goytisolo's apprehension of the concept as revealed in his essays and interviews signals various contradictions with structuralist thought.

The Formalist Critique of Literary History and Influence

Structuralism and its precursor, formalism, questioned many notions that, in the nineteenth century, were held as basic to the study of literature. Two of the most fundamental of these were seminal concepts that remain crucial to many critics today: literary history and influence. These aspects of literary studies derive from a romantic concept of literature as a reflection of a "national spirit," a force that manifests itself through a variety of human phenomena: race, politics, and history, as well as literature. In this view, literary study was a branch of philology, a discipline that sought to understand the totality of civilization. Later nineteenth-century ideologies such as positivism, as expressed in the theories of Hippolyte Taine (1828–1893), used literature to determine the precise environmental and hereditary phenomena that made up the collective psychological state of a given society. In Taine, as in the romantic view, the relationship between the work of art and society was one of cause and effect: literature reflected a national, geographical, or even racial consciousness. Thus the progression of literature through time (literary history) was integrally linked to the social and historical progression of a nation. Similarly, the notion of influence involved the manner in which an author transcribed his or her life experience (a personal relationship with another writer, participation in a political activity, religious training) into the written text. An author was seen as a product of the society in which he or she lived and thus as an embodiment of national and social forces.[5]

At the beginning of this century, the school of Russian formalism reappraised the study of literary history and influence that had dominated the nineteenth century and still permeates literary studies today. Boris Eichenbaum, Victor Shklovsky, and Yuri Tynyanov, among others, asked important questions that challenged many established nineteenth-century concepts. These critics sought to understand the precise relationship between literature and history. They were dubious about the conception of literary progression as a movement toward an ultimate goal, and they criticized literary historians for not coming to terms with their own assumptions. According to Eichenbaum, it was an error to speak of a history of literature that was based on the biographies of authors and on their relationships to political events. Such endeavors told a critic nothing about the dynamics of literature itself, the manner in which forms changed and sparked certain alterations. Shklovsky wrote of a "dialectical self-generation of new forms" in an attempt to divorce himself from the mechanical notion of social reflection that dominated most literary studies at that time. In like manner, Tynyanov tried to understand the evolution of literature as a struggle among certain aesthetic elements. He wrote:

> When people talk about "literary tradition" or "succession" . . . they usually imagine a kind of straight line joining a younger representative of a given literary branch with an older one. As it happens, things are much more complex than that. It is not a matter of continuing on a straight line, but rather one of setting out and pushing off from a given point—a struggle . . . Each instance of literary succession is first and foremost a struggle involving a destruction of the old unity and a new construction out of the old elements.[6]

Tynyanov called the interrelationship between the old and the new elements "the constructional function of a given element" (p. 68). The literary work was seen as a system unto itself, a system that existed within a broader framework of literature. The history of literature could be studied according to what Tynyanov called the auto-function (the relationships between elements of different works) and the syn-function (the relationships between elements of the same work). The general literary system was the ruling factor that conditioned specific literary elements; in other words, the auto-function molded and shaped the syn-function. The changes that literature had undergone through time were regulated by such relationships.

The problem of influence was also pertinent to that of the relationship between social and literary history. Influence studies analyzed the modifications of literature by society, that is, the way in which a literary work was affected by nonliterary phenomena (for example, a political event, a scientific discovery, or a direct encounter between authors). The Russian formalists, however, saw no need to analyze the effects of major social forces on a work of art. They felt that the study of direct contact among authors and of how those personal relationships affected a work had no bearing on the evolution of literature. Influence studies were to be subordinated to the analysis of what Tynyanov called "functional coincidence" (p. 76), the study of literary motifs, conventions, and themes that have appeared throughout the literature of all cultures, regardless of geography or history. The Russian formalists saw the concept of influence as another indication that the traditional approach to literary history was inadequate. In an essay entitled "Literary Environment," Eichenbaum disdainfully remarked: "The traditional literary-historical system was forged without the fundamental distinction between the concepts of genesis and evolution . . . Likewise it made do without attempting to establish what was meant by literary-historical fact. The consequence was a naive theory of 'linear descent' and 'influence,' and an equally naive psychological biographism" (p. 59).

The Russian formalists were also concerned with the precise

relationship between the system of literature and other systems. The conflicting views of this issue held by the critics of the formalists sparked an important polemic in the wake of the revolution in Russia. The formalists were attacked from two angles: by traditional scholars who accused them of being myopic and of ignoring the broader issues of which literature is merely one aspect; and by Marxists who held that the formalists' premises were idealistic. One of the leaders of this second group, Leon Trotsky, conceded that the formalists were adept at clarifying "the artistic and psychological peculiarities of form," yet what he called their "Kantian assumptions" prohibited them from understanding why and how a given tendency in art originated in a given period of history. The formalists, on the other hand, held that the work of art could not be reduced to a mere social and economic object.[7] It is important to stress that some formalists (Tynyanov among them) did not deny the existence of a relationship between literature and society; they wished, however, to formulate a sociological theory of literature that did not exclude aesthetic considerations. Tynyanov argued that the literary system had its own laws as did other systems (politics, history, economics) and that the interrelationships among those systems always had to be considered according to the rules of each autonomous system: "A literary system is first of all a system of the functions of literary order which are in continual interrelationship with other systems" (p. 73). The constitution of this interrelationship was based on social conventions, and the prime mediator between literature and social conventions was language.

From Influence to Intertextuality

It is difficult to pinpoint precisely where formalism stops and structuralism begins; obviously, they overlap. However, Tynyanov's concept of language as a "mediator" is a good point of demarcation. Some formalists had already stressed the importance of linguistics in the study of literature. Tynyanov had written essays in conjunction with Roman Jakobson, who is now considered to be a pioneer in the use of structuralist linguistics in the analysis of literary texts. For Jakobson, linguistics—the system of language—was a model for literary studies. Just as a sentence is an embodiment of certain laws that govern the order of words, a literary text is a concrete manifestation of the rules that apply to the system of literature. Jakobson stressed what he called "literariness," the essence of literature, the elements of the text that act out the conventions and strategies of literature.

The systematization of literature begun by the formalists and carried to its full consequences by the structuralists has acquired new vitality in the last three decades and has continued to question the assumptions of traditional critics. One of the important problems raised by the structuralists is the notion of authorship. Nineteenth-century literary-history and influence studies were based on the view that the author was the single creator of the text—the text's only source. Structuralist critics and theoreticians, however, seek to focus attention away from the author and toward the conventions involved in the processes of writing and reading.

These conventions function on an unconscious level as does the system of language itself. We are not aware, for example, of the phonological rules of our language when we speak. Because speaking, writing, and reading are unconscious processes, structuralists reject the view of the self or the subject as that which gives meaning to the world. In Jonathan Culler's words, "structural explanation does not place a certain action in a causal chain nor derive it from the project by which a subject intends a world; it relates the object or action to a system of conventions which give it its meaning and distinguish it from other phenomena with different meanings. Something is explained by the system of distinctions which give it its identity."[8] This idea of the self, the "I" that, from Descartes's *cogito* to Sartre's existentialism, has identified consciousness, becomes in structuralist thought the construct of systems of conventions and cultural patterns: "the 'I' is not given but comes to exist."[9] To think of the author as the source of his or her work is, in effect, to affirm the view of the self that structuralism rejects. An author cannot be the defining principle of the work of art, for he or she must operate according to a previously existing system. When an author writes, he or she assumes the existence of readers who are able to employ that system for their own purposes.

Such a radical break with one of the most basic concepts in the study of literature, the notion of authorship, has great bearing on the problems of literary history and influence. It is no longer essential to trace the literary development of a nation from author to author nor even to prove the influence of one writer on another. Literature constantly imitates itself, learns from its previous designs, and incorporates them into "new" constructs.

As structuralists reassessed the status of the author, the subject who single-handedly created a work as a result of an encounter with the world, they were led to the idea of *text,* a physical object produced through the assimilation and incorporation of conventions. A text is, in this view, the product of the activities of writing and reading.

In one of her early works, Julia Kristeva defines *text* as

> un appareil translinguistique qui redistribue l'ordre de la langue, . . . Le texte est donc une PRODUCTIVITÉ, ce qui veut dire: (1) son rapport à la langue dans laquelle il se situe est redistributif (destructivo-constructif), par conséquent il est abordable à travers des catégories logiques et mathématiques plutôt que purement linguistiques; (2) il est une permutation de textes, une inter-textualité: dans l'espace d'un texte plusieurs énoncés, pris à d'autres textes, se croisent et se neutralisent.

> (a translinguistic mechanism that redistributes the order of language *(langue)* . . . The text is therefore a productivity, which means: (1) its relationship to the language *(langue)* in which it is found is redistributory (destructive-constructive), consequently it can be approached through logical and mathematical categories rather than purely linguistic ones; (2) it is a permutation of texts, an intertextuality: within the space of one text many utterances, taken from other texts, intersect and neutralize each other.)[10]

This concept of text already contains the subject at hand —intertextuality. When critics analyze relationships between texts, the presence of one or various texts within another, they set aside the psychological concept of influence and advance a very different view not only of the specific work but also of literature itself. In this view, the recurrence of a literary phenomenon is the result, not of influence, but of texts making contact with one another, reproducing, and struggling in a constant state of interaction. This re-creation is a vital part of literature rather than an occasional aberration of the normally individual creative process, as the accepted use of the word *influence* implies.

In addition to influence, intertextuality also involves another literary concept—the real. For structuralists, realism is, in many ways, a misnomer if one considers one of the central premises in Saussurian linguistics: the formula of the arbitrariness of the sign. According to Ferdinand de Saussure,[11] there is nothing intrinsic within a linguistic sign that allows us to connect the real object to which that sign refers with the sign itself. The phonic or graphic constituents of a word enter into a relationship with the concept of the word: the sign as a whole is equivalent to its form (its signifier) plus its meaning (its signified). Poststructuralists elucidate the notion of sign by pointing out its fundamental incompleteness.[12] We can never truly reach the reality of an object through language; we can only grasp it conceptually. When critics speak of "realism" in literature, they must keep in mind that words can never directly reflect objects; they only mediate the relationship between our idea or mental construct of reality and reality itself. Realism in its most naive sense is, as Tzvetan Todorov says, an attempt to forget language, to act as if words were merely the docile names of things.[13] Barthes similarly situates the problem of the real within the context of codes. In his intricate analysis of *Sarrasine,* a relatively minor story by Honoré de Balzac, Barthes discusses the impossibility of performing in reality certain actions that take place in the story. He submits that "discourse has no responsibility vis-à-vis the real: in the most realistic novel, the referent has no 'reality.' . . . what we call 'real' (in the theory of the realist text) is never more than a code of representation (of signification): it is never a code of execution: *the novelistic real is not operable.*"[14]

These views of *vraisemblance* ("verisimilitude") strongly suggest the idea of intertextuality: to approach the real in literature is to enter into a relationship with other texts. Intertextuality is thus the basic concept in the structuralist view of literature, for it is seen as a mediation between the text and the world outside it. In this scheme, the world becomes a series of texts, and any attempt to write presupposes the borrowing of any one or more of these texts and incorporating it or them into the script. Kristeva, who among literary theorists offers the most detailed theory of intertextuality, has articulated this relationship between the world and the text. In an article, "Problèmes de la structuration du texte" ("Problems in the Structuring of the Text"),[15] she places what have been considered types of nonliterary discourse (politics, journalism) within the category of literature. In this analysis, all discourse that offers information employs a system of codes as does literature. She states at one point that semiology treats literature in the same way as it does a news story or a scientific essay because all these texts engage in the "practice of signifying" (p. 298). This idea of practice or productivity of signification is reaffirmed in her definition of *text,* which is repeated nearly word for word from the discussion in *Le texte du roman (The Text of the Novel)*. Literature and discourse both fall under the heading of text, a phenomenon that redistributes the order of language *(langue)* as well as the order of previous texts ("il est une permutation de textes").

This constant reproduction of previous texts is further seen as having ideological ramifications. Since the definition of *text* takes in such a wide variety of factors (history, science, culture), it allows Kristeva to pose textual interplay (intertextuality) as a mediation between the text and the world outside it, between the literary and the real, between literature and life. In *Le texte du roman,* she states that intertextuality is a concept that designates the manner in which the text reads history and places itself in a historical context. The concrete manifestation of intertextuality in a specific text provides the principal social framework of the text itself (p. 311). She later employs the term *idéologème* to describe the manner in which the text interacts with society. *Idéologème* is the function that links outside structures to an internal one: the inclusion of scientific discourse, for example, within a novel. There is a distinction between the accepted notion of ideology, which interprets society and history according to certain interests, and *idéologème,* in which there is a purely semiological relationship between the words (signs) of two or more texts. In *Le texte du roman* she argues that the acceptance of the notion of *idéologème* allows semiology to deal with the text in relation to *the texts of* society and history (p. 12; my italics). Such an analysis leads Kristeva to break down the relationship even further with her discussion of the *idéologème du signe.* If signs are the basic constituents of texts, the same interactions that take place among texts must also take place among signs. The consequences of this idea are far-reaching for Kristeva. The *idéologème du signe* makes for constant semiotic transformations and mutations, for a regeneration of words. The dependence on the word as a static entity is, for Kristeva, an affirmation of the universal, of the ideal, of God. She gives the word a dynamic entity that is defined not by its essence but by its active capabilities for infinite associations. Thus intertextuality with all its manifestations is for Kristeva a principle that represents a new way of perceiving literature as well as the world.

While Kristeva's conception of intertextuality is part of a larger philosophical enterprise, Barthes limits his occasional commentaries on intertextuality to purely literary matters. Barthes's principal contribution to the discussion is his analysis of the reader and his or her relationship to the text. If the author's creation of a text necessarily involves the absorption and modification of other texts (a Kristevian idea that Barthes accepts), it follows that a work must be read in conjunction with a set of previous literary experiences. In *S/Z,* we see that Balzac's story may be subjected to a plurality of readings that create not only a plurality of texts but also a plurality of readers. Barthes's reader is not a single, specific entity who personally encounters a work of literature but the manifestation of a collective experience that shapes and determines the way that we approach a text: "This 'I' [the reader] . . . is already a plurality of other texts, of codes which are infinite or, more precisely, lost (whose origin is lost) . . . [The 'I'] is the wake of all codes which constitute me, so that my subjectivity has ultimately the generality of stereotypes."[16] Yet Barthes's view of reading is always active. He writes of the activity of reading in terms of a "labor." "To read, in fact, is a labor of language. To read is to find meanings, and to find meanings is to name them; but these named meanings are swept toward other names; names call to each other, reassemble, and their grouping calls for further naming."[17] We are reminded of Kristeva's attempt to break down textual interaction to semiological interaction. Barthes activates Kristeva's idea by subjecting it to the dynamic process of reading or "naming and re-naming." In *The Pleasure of the Text* we find a similar concept advanced through Barthes's constant use of the first person as he poses himself as the reader of texts. For example, in a section devoted specifically to intertextuality, Barthes (or the "I") detects the presence of Marcel Proust in a work by Gustave Flaubert. Proust's writing serves as the reference material on which an episode of Flaubert's *Mémoires d'un touriste* is based even though Proust is the later of the two authors. Barthes is able to label (name) Flaubert's text according to Proust because the "I" is already made up of all previous texts to which it has been exposed.[18]

For Barthes, as for Kristeva, intertextuality is an all-encompassing concept whose consequences transcend a reading of any one text. Both theoreticians' constant insistence on the plurality of texts and significations implies a deep rejection of any attempt to single out one reading as having greater validity than any other. Such an endeavor is, in Barthes's words, the same as "stopping the chain of systems." To establish a "singular theological meaning" of a text is precisely what Barthes as well as Kristeva militantly refuse to do. This posture toward literature suggests a philosophical position that is intricately pursued in Kristeva's discourse in which literary criticism and philosophy have been synthesized in an attempt to break with the accepted concepts and methods of perception inherent in the occidental tradition. The totality of Kristeva's project presents problems for those of us primarily concerned with literature.

Questions immediately arise when we attempt to apply the concept to a particular text. Is intertextuality necessarily a theoretical problem, or is it a specific issue on which we can focus the discussion of one text? In other words, is intertextuality an all-encompassing idea that pertains to the totality of literature, or is it a formal device, an artistic tool employed by a writer to create a certain limited effect? While for Kristeva and Barthes intertextuality is a concept in literary theory, the critic who wishes to analyze its presence in the work of a single author must deal with specific instances of the phenomenon. Citation, plagiarism, and imitation are all particular aspects of intertextuality and all function differently within a work as well as from work to work. Intertextuality may function purely phonetically, stylistically, or semantically. It may take the form of a title or a character from another work. An author may be mentioned, or a film, or any work of art. The text may try to capture the spirit of a previous text by reproducing its themes and motifs. Intertextuality is pertinent to one or to any combination of these specific literary occurrences.

The existence of specific identifiable instances of intertextuality seems to imply that it is a formal device. Some texts are intertextual and others are not; certain passages of a text have intertextual elements while the rest of the text does not. Yet if one considers the consequences of the view of intertextuality put forth by Kristeva and Barthes, isolated occurrences of this phenomenon become subordinate to a total theory of writing. Writing, for these French critics, is the act of arranging and rearranging a system of borrowed codes. The use of language is itself a process of borrowing.

Edward W. Said's penetrating analysis of the activity of writing further illustrates the dependence of authors on other authors. His definition of *text* is similar to that of Kristeva in his advancement of the text as a procreator or a father. Texts are themselves "beginnings" because they serve as incitations or inspirations for other texts. "Since there is no such thing as an absolutely primal text, each act of composition involves other texts, and so each writing transmits itself, receives other writing, is an interpretation of other writing, reconstitutes by displacement other writing."[19] Said goes on to characterize the modern writer (his examples include Stephen Mallarmé, Oscar Wilde, and Jorge Luis Borges) as one who is actively aware of this aspect of his or her own production.

The trend in the literature of this century toward self-awareness—the writer's consciousness of his or her own activity and his or her explicit reference to that process—is another problematical issue related to intertextuality. Self-reflection or self-referentiality is, according to Barthes, modern literature's most salient characteristic, a way of probing into its own designs.[20] Placed within the context of intertextuality, the phenomenon of self-reflection presents a new series of problems. The interest in self-reflection in structuralist and poststructuralist criticism has not, strangely enough, produced a great deal of analysis relating the two issues. Kristeva's *Le texte du roman* touches on the relationship but does not discuss it in detail. In that early work, Kristeva points out that a reference to another written text has two important consequences. First, there is a transformation of temporality. The writing no longer refers to a time outside of the text; rather the narrative sequences are oriented toward the activity of writing itself, "the movement of the hand over the page." Second, the written text and the citation (or the reference to the other written text) together form another text that presents itself as a totality, as "an object of exchange" (p. 148). These transformations allow the written text to reflect the instance of the writing, and in so doing, the text lays bare its desire for self-discovery. In this analysis, Kristeva begins the development of an idea that has bearing on an essential aspect of intertextuality, but she puts off its further elaboration.

Lucien Dällenbach, another French theoretician, continues the discussion in "Intertexte et autotexte," an article that is an amplification of several issues in his book on self-reflection in literature, *Le récit spéculaire: Essai sur le mise en abyme*.[21] In his article, Dällenbach distinguishes between two types of intertextuality: *external intertextuality,* the relationship of one text to another; and *internal intertextuality,* the internal relationships within the text itself (p. 282). The latter phenomenon is named *intertextualité autarcique* or *autotextualité.* Autotextuality is, in Dällenbach's scheme, capable of creating what he calls a *mise en abyme,* a textual mirror in which we perceive the text's reflection of itself. Thus, according to Dällenbach, autotextuality is a subcategory of intertextuality. It is significant that Dällenbach places both internal and external relationships among texts within a context of intertextuality. Intertextuality thus encompasses any textual relationship, any instance in literature in which a text carries on a dialogue with another text or with itself. Thus Dällenbach's concept of the *mise en abyme* allows the text that is being written to become an intertext.

The theoretical problems contained in the concept of intertextuality are also treated in the fictional works of modern writers who display an awareness of their own activity as they write. Borges, Robbe-Grillet, Octavio Paz, and Thomas Pynchon, to name a few, have made implicit or explicit statements not only on their own writing but also on the act of writing in general. Such awareness makes for an acute consciousness of the origins or sources of their writing—where and how they acquired their material. Thus intertextuality is used by these authors as a literary device and as a means of probing into their own process of writing. In the hands of these authors, a text becomes a statement on its own genesis. This trend in modern literature implies a concerted effort to bridge the gap between theory and fiction; each literary text is seen as a critical commentary on its own development. Barthes has pointed out the tendency in modern literature to uncover its own origins in language:

> For centuries, our writers did not imagine it was possible to consider literature (the word itself is recent) as a language, subject, like any other, to logical distinction: literature never reflected upon itself

(sometimes upon its figures, but never upon its being), it never divided itself into an object at once scrutinizing and scrutinized; in short, it spoke but did not speak itself. And then, probably with the first shocks to the good conscience of the bourgeoisie, literature began to regard itself as double: at once object and scrutiny of that object, utterance and utterance of that utterance, literature-object and meta-literature.[22]

Yet the "doubling" of literature into subject and object may also be seen as an integration, as a convergence of literature and discourse on literature. The most revealing examples of this phenomenon can be found in contemporary Latin American novels. The feature that is perhaps most distinctive to these novels is precisely the attempt to bridge the gap between theory and practice, between the writing of fiction and the commentary on fiction. Typical of this endeavor are the works of Severo Sarduy. His essays are consciously structured along the lines of a modern work of fiction. They are filled with devices that are generally accepted as exclusive to literature (dialogue, proliferation of metaphor, incomplete sentences, the creation of fictitious characters).[23] His works of fiction, however, employ conventions that are appropriate to criticism, such as the frequent use of footnotes in *Cobra*.

Sarduy's conception of intertextuality is subsumed under his theory of the baroque and the neobaroque, a crucial issue in the contemporary Latin American novel. Sarduy and other Hispanic writers of his generation (Guillermo Cabrera Infante, Carlos Fuentes, and Goytisolo) conceive of the baroque literature of seventeenth-century Spain as a model for their own writing. In this context, Luis de Góngora is seen as the master of a style that liberates words from a finite number of significations as they regenerate new forms both semantically and phonetically. Sarduy opens his essay on the baroque with:

> Lo barroco estaba destinado, desde su nacimiento, a la ambigüedad, a la difusión semántica. Fue la gruesa perla irregular—en español barrueco o berrueco, en portugués barroco—, la roca, lo nudose, la densidad aglutinada de la piedra—barrueco o berrueco—, quizá la excrecencia, el quiste, lo que prolifera, al mismo tiempo libre y lítico, tumoral, verrugoso. (p. 167)

(Since its birth, the baroque was destined to ambiguity, to semantic diffusion. It was the thick irregular pearl—in Spanish *barrueco* or *berrueco,* in Portuguese, *barroco*—the rock, that which is knotted, the coagulated density of the rock—perhaps excrescence, a cyst, that which proliferates, at once liberated and lithic, tumorlike, warty.)

Sarduy's description is itself written in a baroque style; his writing becomes what he attempts to define. In his description, the baroque is characterized as a distancing of the signified from its signifier through a substitution of other signifiers. The result is an endless chain of meanings in which the text becomes swollen with an infinite number of possible readings. In Sarduy's words (p. 170), this type of baroque "consiste en obliterar el significante de un significado dado pero no remplazándolo por otro, por distante que éste se encuentre del primero, sino por una cadena de significantes que progresa metonímicamente y que termina circunscribiendo al significante ausente" ("consists of obliterating the signifier of a given signified and replacing it not with another signified, but with a chain of signifiers that progresses metonymically and ends up circumscribing the absent signifier"). According to this scheme, intertextuality is the mechanism by which words refer to other words from other texts. Thus the baroque is characterized by intertextuality. Sarduy pinpoints two distinct categories: citation, the actual incorporation of specific texts within another; and reminiscence, the latent traces of cultural and historical phenomena that are deeply ingrained within a society.

Sarduy's theory of intertextuality reminds us of Kristeva's attempt to place a text in relation to other social and historical texts (her notion of *idéologème*). In both, human experience that is put into language is considered not as a unique text but as a mosaic of texts. In *Escrito sobre un cuerpo* (p. 66), Sarduy analyzes the baroque writing of Lezama Lima: "Texto que se repite, que se cita sin límites, que se plagia a sí mismo; tapiz que se desteje para hilar otros signos, . . . La literatura sin fronteras históricas ni lingüísticas" ("Text that repeats itself, that cites itself, that plagiarizes itself, a tapestry that is unstrung in order to weave other signs, . . . Literature without historical or linguistic boundaries"). We see in these words not only a description of Lezama's *Paraíso* but also a vision of literature in which the primary agent, the element that sets a process into motion, is not a human being (the author) but language. For Kristeva and Barthes (who are representatives of contemporary critical theory) as well as for Sarduy (who is typical of the theory and practice of modern concepts in aesthetics), the author's status as the sole owner of his or her creation fades as the text reemerges and takes on new vitality.

The concepts of literary theory discussed by figures such as Kristeva, Barthes, Dällenbach, and Sarduy, especially intertextuality, are of particular importance to Juan Goytisolo, the young Spaniard who moves to Paris intent on making his mark on world literature. Intertextuality, autotextuality (or self-consciousness), the supremacy of the text over the author, the real are all notions with which Goytisolo becomes familiar and feels he must confront and, at times, assimilate. But, as we shall see, familiarization and assimilation are paradoxical, for the guiding force behind this new Parisian Goytisolo is the oppression and rancid literary legacy of sacred Spain.

2. Intertextuality and Juan Goytisolo

Goytisolo's conception of writing poses interesting problems. At first glance, the intertextual nature of his later works and the explicit commentaries on intertextuality in his essays reveal a marked affinity among Goytisolo, modern French theorists such as Julia Kristeva and Roland Barthes, and contemporary Latin American novelists such as Severo Sarduy. But at the same time, there are elements in Goytisolo's writing that place him at odds with both groups. This contradiction is crucial to Goytisolo's novelistic enterprise.[1]

Goytisolo considers himself closer to Latin American novelists and poets than to the peninsular writers of his own generation. Stylistic and linguistic similarities (the use of the *tú* and the future tense) are not the only factors that link him to the Latin Americans, for behind the formal resemblance lies a conception of writing shared by authors from Hispanic America. Sarduy's attempt to "obliterate the signifier from the signified," for example, is a manifestation of a bellicose search for language in which Goytisolo wishes to participate.[2] Although Goytisolo has not written an article solely on intertextuality and his purely theoretical discussions of literature are relatively scarce, he shows (though never explicitly) an awareness in his essays as well as in his fiction that intertextuality leads to basic issues concerning the nature of literature and language.

Goytisolo's familiarity with the concept of intertextuality is apparent in several interviews in which he elucidates his relationship with other writers and texts as well as with the whole of the Hispanic literary tradition. In these interviews Goytisolo offers general definitions that resemble the Kristevan concept of intertextuality. In a discussion of his own writing, Goytisolo mentions the term *intertextuality* when he describes his attempt to carry on a dialogue in which the "voices" of other texts rebound off one another and enter into a relationship with the author, who is in turn represented by another voice.[3] Elsewhere, in the form of a "Declaration" made during a symposium on the contemporary peninsular novel, he speaks of one of his later novels, *Reivindicación del Conde don Julián*. He explains to his audience that the citations of different Spanish authors from the Middle Ages to the present day function in *Don Julián* in the same way as do descriptions of scenery and people in ordinary novels. *Don Julián* is described as a text that is nourished by the living matter of other texts. This intertextual endeavor is part of the Cervantine legacy. *Don Quijote,* he goes on to say, is a response to books of chivalry and, at times, to the pastoral novel. It is also a satire of Lope de Vega. According to Goytisolo, the most interesting aspect of Cervantes's work is that it comments on itself and on rival genres as it creates a new one.[4]

These declarations reveal Goytisolo's awareness of the issue, but they also show a rather hazy analysis of the problem. In fact, it is difficult to ascertain exactly how he grasps the term or if he understands it at all. For some critics, his distinction between "esta novela" (his own, which is like that of Cervantes) and "las novelas ordinarias" would appear superficial. Is Goytisolo's view limited to a reading of certain texts that he designates as being intertextual? Does his analysis of *Don Quijote* imply a theory of normative aesthetics, a view that modern critics tend to reject? Or is Goytisolo describing a willingness on the part of modern writers (himself included) to incorporate their own readings of the "classic" texts such as *Don Quijote* into their own writing?

One of the essays in *Disidencias,* "Lectura cervantina de *Tres tristes tigres*" ("A Cervantine Reading of *Three Trapped Tigers,*" pp. 193–219), in which he defends Guillermo Cabrera Infante against charges made by critics who said that *TTT* was a disorganized novel, contains a discussion of the intertextual structure of both *Don Quijote* and Cabrera Infante's work. But Goytisolo's apprehension of the concept as expressed in that article is no less muddled than the one in his "Declaration." His central argument in the defense of Cabrera Infante is a comparison, a parallel drawn between the intertextual dialogues in *Don Quijote* and in *TTT*. The contemporary Cuban, whose merit may still be questioned, is placed in the same category with a writer who is considered one of the greatest of all time simply because both make use of the concept of intertextuality. Throughout the essay, Goytisolo refers to an "intertextual play"; at other points, he calls it an "intertextual relation" or an "intertextual dialogue." He goes a bit further in this essay than he did in his "Declaration" when he states that *Don Quijote* is evidence that a text (any text) cannot be studied in isolation, as if it were born of nothing or were a product of the outside world. It must be analyzed in relation to other texts and to the system of values and significations that these texts carry along. At one point, he cites the Russian formalists as the authorities who prove his point (p. 194). But then, in the next pages, he contradicts himself.

> Nadie mejor que Cervantes concocía el valor y originalidad del objeto literario . . . Cervantes se autodefine "raro inventor" y se preocupa por indicarnos *ab initio* que su libro es absolutamente distinto de los que, por aquellas fechas, se publican y obtienen el favor del público; desde el prólogo entabla un diálogo imaginario con el lector medio, desti- nado a poner de relieve el signo diferencial de su novela con respecto al sistema literario de su tiempo. (p. 196)

> (No one knew the value and originality of the literary object more than Cervantes. . . . Cervantes defines himself as a "rare inventor," and takes care to indicate to us *ab initio* that his book is quite unlike those that were published and favorably accepted by the public in those days; throughout the work the author enters into an imaginary dialogue with the reader that differentiates his own work from the literary system of his time.)

The key word in this passage is *originalidad,* an idea that implies a romantic notion of the author as a "raro inventor" whose unique talent allows him or her to create something totally and excitingly new. How then does Goytisolo pose the problem? Does he argue as do the formalists and structuralists that literature can only be created in conjunction with and in response to other literature, or does he continue to advance the old notion of the author as inventor or source? Perhaps he would clarify the point for us, if asked, but the essay, a piece unlike Sarduy's "El barroco y el neo-barroco" in its straightforward, at times pedantic, prose, gives us little help.[5]

Since the specific discussions of intertextuality give rise to a plethora of questions, perhaps we should look elsewhere for Goytisolo's view of the concept. Rather than searching for concrete references to the intertextual process, it may be more beneficial to inspect the underlying assumptions of his literary ideology. First, Goytisolo's conception of intertextuality revolves around an attempt to reevaluate the literary tradition of Spain. *Don Julián,* perhaps the best example, can be read as a re-creation, rereading, and reassessment of texts that have been elevated to the hallowed list of great Spanish works of art. Goytisolo's personal reading or misreading of these texts, his negative appraisal of some of them and his admiration of others, form the basis of his writing.

The synthesis between reading and writing has ideological ramifications. Much has been made of Goytisolo the expatriate, the self-banished Spaniard, and of the thematic aspects of his novels that reflect this condition. But there has been little investigation of the textual interplay that is central to his writing. Goytisolo's aversion for his homeland manifests itself through a reading of certain authors and texts that he considers misunderstood by the majority of Spanish critics. His dissenting posture toward these texts reveals his attitudes toward Spanish society as well as toward its literature. If we inspect the list of writers who are admired by Goytisolo—Fernando de Rojas, Mariano José de Larra, Max Aub, and Luis Cernuda—we note that all have had to cope in one way or another with political, religious, or cultural oppression. Goytisolo reads the texts of these writers as a manifestation of the turmoil and suffering they endured and relates their experiences to his own life.

Of all the facets of Spanish culture and history that Goytisolo sees as characteristic of a theocratic and politically tyrannical society, the most salient is censorship. It is a constant theme in his book of essays, *El furgón de cola,* and it is integrally related to the problems of literature and language that are basic to his writing. Laws prohibiting the dissemination of certain written, auditory, or visual material have far-reaching consequences for Goytisolo. In his view, these laws touch on a variety of issues in the understanding of Spanish culture. In the first series of essays— "La actualidad de Larra" ("Larra Today"), "Escribir en España" ("To Write in Spain"), "Los escritores frente al toro de la censura" ("Writers against the Censor's Bull"), "La literatura perseguida por la política" ("The Persecution of Literature by Politics"), and "Literatura y eutanasia" ("Literature and Euthanasia")— Goytisolo discusses the direct results of censorship in terms of the relationship between literature and society, especially in the post-civil-war Spanish novel. Censorship and self-censorship necessarily situate all that is written within a political arena. The writer is by definition engaged in politics because the act of writing always has the potential of becoming a threat to the established order. Goytisolo, however, wants to go beyond a mere thematic criticism of the intolerance of the regime because he believes that denouncing a dictatorship by using the same rhetoric as that of the regime is not a radical enterprise. One must attack the rhetoric itself: invade, subvert, and destroy it. He argues, in effect (p. 56), that the criticism must become intertextual (even though he does not employ the term specifically): "Nuestro anquilosado lenguaje castellanista exige, en efecto, con urgencia, el uso de la dinamita o el purgante. El futuro renovador de nuestra narrativa será aquel, creo yo, que corte más audazmente sus amarras con el pesado lastre de la tradición que soportamos" ("Our arthritic Castilian [Castilianist] language urgently demands, in effect, the use of dynamite or a purgative. The renovating future of our narrative, I think, will consist of writing that boldly severs its ties with the weighty and stifling tradition we must endure"). The "tradition we must endure" is not simply the cultural legacy of Spain; it includes the texts that manifest that legacy. To attack censorship as effectively as possible is, therefore, to confront the language of censorship, to rediscover the silence that the laws have produced.

Much of *El furgón* consists of essays on specific Spanish writers, including historical figures such as Bartolomé de las Casas. There is a significant dichotomy between the few whom Goytisolo reveres and those whose high reputation he questions and ultimately attacks. Goytisolo's personal reading or misreading of these authors and his categorization of them allow him to make use of their texts in his own literary creation. Representative of this division is the polarization between Cernuda and the writers of the Generation of '98 (above all, Miguel de Unamuno, Azorín [José Martínez Ruiz], and Antonio Machado). Goytisolo reads Cernuda as "un español sin ganas de serlo" ("a Spaniard who wishes he weren't") and sees in Cernuda's poetry the same anxieties and tensions that spark *Don Julián* and *Juan sin tierra*. The motif of destruction, a constant in both of these works, is taken from Cernuda's poem "Limbo," the last line of which reads, "Mejor la destrucción, el fuego" ("Better [to choose] destruction, fire"). Cernuda's treatment at the hands of Spanish literary critics is the cause of much anger and hostility on Goytisolo's part. In his eyes, Cernuda's importance has been downgraded by post-civil-war criticism for ideological reasons. The threat to the regime seen in poets such as Rafael Alberti, Miguel Hernández, and Cernuda impels the literary critics of the establishment to ignore them. For this reason, there has been undue emphasis placed on a "safer" group of writers—the Generation of '98. In an essay, "La herencia del noventa y ocho" ("The Legacy of '98"), Goytisolo writes of the glorification of this group of authors. He submits (p. 70) that the indiscriminate adoration of both *modernistas* and the figures of 1898 results in a sterile and paralyzing criticism, literary studies that are blind to a new generation of writers, himself included, whose desires and interests are diametrically opposed to those of their predecessors. Thus it is not so much that certain writers are viewed with repulsion but that the Generation of '98 has been excessively revered and mythified. Goytisolo takes it on himself to destroy that myth, to penetrate the texts of the "masters," and to pull the pedestals out from under them.

The theoretical implications behind Goytisolo's reading of the Spanish literary tradition lead to an understanding of intertextuality as a formal device, as a means of expressing a personal attitude toward that tradition. The specificity of this concept, however, cannot be accepted without the consideration of other implications. The creation of textual and vital bonds between authors, such as those between Cernuda and Goytisolo, implies a notion of intertextuality as self-reading. Even authors and texts that Goytisolo views negatively can become his foils, his mirror-texts, for they manifest a diametric opposition between Goytisolo and the Spanish literary tradition. Throughout *Señas, Don Julián,* and *Juan sin tierra,* there is an attempt to create hostile relationships between texts in the form of parodies and ironic assertions about the "wondrous" cultural achievements of the Spanish nation. No less interesting in this respect is the identification of the outside texts (as in the case of Cernuda's poetry) with those of Goytisolo. In these instances, the outside texts also become mirrors reflecting Goytisolo's own designs.

The most telling example of self-reading is Goytisolo's analysis of José María Blanco White.[6] This early nineteenth-century, self-exiled essayist struggled against the oppressive Spanish political climate under Fernando VII, and for this reason, Goytisolo argues, he has largely remained neglected and misunderstood. In Goytisolo's view, Blanco was far ahead of his time. His critique of Spain and his religious uncertainties extended beyond the liberalism of most Spanish intellectuals of that period in that his conclusions were always, in Goytisolo's view, ambiguous. After relating the hardships and existential turmoil imposed on Blanco through the condition of exile, Goytisolo describes the world view to which such suffering necessarily leads. The only possible conclusion, he tells us, for a man like Blanco who is gifted with a critical spirit, is that no conclusion is possible (p. 20). Yet Goytisolo qualifies this interpretation of Blanco with the words *parece decirnos* ("[Blanco] seems to tell us"). This disclaimer unveils the tension in Goytisolo's self-reading, an awareness of his own misreading. Later in

the essay, the self-reading becomes explicit as Goytisolo transforms his study into a first-person account of the ideology of
expatriatism. He states that all patriotic values are alien to him,
that very little, if anything, that has to do with official Spain is
agreeable to him. On the contrary, sacred Spain is repugnant to
Goytisolo; his repugnance has been born of a long process of
displacement and dispossession (pp. 96–97). In the same paragraph he speaks of the failure of Spanish liberalism, stating that
the defeat of the forces of human progress has led the most lucid
and visionary Spaniards to confront the history of their nation
and to affirm their own destiny in opposition to the traditional
forces of the peninsula (p. 97). Blanco did just that, according to
Goytisolo, and that is also what he, the author of *Don Julián,*
tries to do in his writing. Blanco, the personality, the figure, has
become a text in which Goytisolo sees his own reflection.

    The literary figure as text or mirror-text is best seen in an
instance of Goytisolo's essayistic production in which the intertextual process lays itself bare to the reader. In one of the briefest
but most gripping essays in *El furgón,* "Escribir en España,"
Goytisolo's irony is dependent on Larra's. The topic is not Larra
per se but political repression. Larra's voice resounds, however,
throughout the essay in the form of ironic praise of Spanish
censorship, which at first glance seems to hail the benefits of
Spain's political situation under the Franco regime. The article is
structured around a first-person narrator (a device often used by
Larra) who attempts to answer the opinion voiced by a Parisian
that Spaniards are fortunate to be under the wing of censorship
because they have something concrete to struggle against, unlike
the French whose social criticism is always watered down by the
appearance of political tolerance. Struck by the assertion, the
narrator gives in to his own chauvinistic attitudes and declares
that, after a long period of deep reflection, he is inclined to believe
that the Parisian's words point to an inescapable truth (p. 22).
These words are followed by reasoned arguments whose conclusion leads one to believe that censorship is the underlying force
behind the greatness of Spanish letters.

De los lejanos tiempos en que los inquisidores de fray Tomás de Torquemada enviaban a la hoguera a todos los sospechosos de herejía o judaísmo hasta la actual reglamentación del Ministerio de Información y Turismo, la censura española ha adquirido un proceso capital de experiencia que ningún descontento (es triste, pero todavía los hay) pudiera negarle. Hoy día ya no se quema a los escritores en la plaza pública (como en los siglos XVI, XVII, XVIII) ni siquiera sus obras (como en el siglo XIX y aún en fecha muy reciente) sin que por ello esta institución (origen y guía de las que hoy se multiplican por el mundo) haya perdido un ápice de su fuerza y de su juventud. A un francés nuestra pequeña vanidad nacional se le antojará probablemente ridícula pero, a nosotros, escritores españoles, con cuarto siglos de Inquisición encima, la actual legislación de nuestros censores que nos garantiza la vida, a veces el reposo forzado y, en cualquier caso, el silencio nos llena de entusiasmo. (pp. 22–23)

(From the ancient days of the inquisitors when Friar Tomás de Torquemada sentenced those under the suspicion of heresy or Judaism to a fiery death until today's administration of the Ministry of Information and Tourism, Spanish censorship has acquired a level of expertise that no malcontent (it's sad, but there are still a few) can deny. Today's writers are not publicly burned at the stake, as they were in the sixteenth, seventeenth, and eighteenth centuries. Their works are not even burned, as they were in the nineteenth and the present centuries. This does not mean, however, that our institution (a model for so many others throughout the world) has lost one iota of youthful vitality. To a Frenchman our little national vanity may seem ridiculous, but to us Spanish writers with four centuries of Inquisition under our belts, the present-day censorship laws guarantee us everlasting life, sometimes a long-needed rest, and, in any case, the silence fills our hearts with enthusiasm.)

The evocation of Larra is revealed not only through an allusion to a specific text but also through the imitation of Larra's style. The highly rhetorical treatment of Spanish history, the comparison between Spain and an enlightened Europe (in this case, France),[7] and the ironic interplay between the grandeur, on the one hand, and the anachronistic nature of Spanish culture, on the other, are all ways of creating a bond between Larra's language and that of Goytisolo. The narrator's aversion for the malcontents is also present in a Larra essay, "Lo que no se puede decir" ("That Which Cannot Be Said"): "Una cosa que aborrezco [es] . . . esos hombres naturalmente turbulentos que se alimentan de oposición, ... esos hombres que quieren que las guerras no duren, que se acaben pronto las facciones, que haya libertad de imprenta" ("One thing that I abhor [is] those men who are by nature contrary, those who find nourishment from opposition ... those men who want wars and animosity to end, those who want freedom of the press").[8] In like manner, the ironic tribute to the grandiose accomplishments of Spanish censorship in Goytisolo's essay can be seen in Larra's article, "La alabanza" ("Praise"), in which Larra affirms that the purpose of censorship is to assure that all that is written is true: "¿Qué censor había de prohibir la *verdad*, y qué Gobierno ilustrado, como el nuestro, no la había de querer oír ... para mentir, más vale no escribir" ("What censor could possibly prohibit truth? And what enlightened government (like ours) would not want to hear it? ... If one wishes to lie, better not write anything at all").[9] The intertextual nature of Goytisolo's essay becomes highly elaborate as the narrator actually quotes from the essay on praise in which Larra sardonically declares (p. 25) that praise must be allowed at all cost because a laudatory remark could never be excessive, " 'sobre todo para el alabado' " (" 'especially for the one who is being praised' "). And further we find (p. 26): "Como decía Larra: '¿Puede haber nada más hermoso ni más pacífico que un país en el que no se habla?' " ("As Larra said: 'Can there be anything in the world more beautiful or more harmoniously tranquil than a country in which no one speaks?' "). Larra's words, ironic in the original text, are employed by the narrator as serious statements. Besides being a device in the critique of censorship, the presence of Larra in this essay is a comment on intertextuality: it affirms the possibilities of a textual dialogue in which the texts reflect each other.

The theoretical problems posed by Goytisolo in the specific intertextual process that he adopts remain open. He offers no solutions for the theorist. The simplistic and self-contradictory discussions of intertextuality as a theoretical principle are rendered complex only in the context of Goytisolo's total literary enterprise. Kristeva's concept of intertextuality as an integral aspect of all writing and of all texts seems not to concur with Goytisolo's conception of intertextuality as a method of destroying a culture and re-creating it. Even Kristeva's notion of *idéologème* is at odds with it because her category is still a universal concept. Goytisolo's conception of the intertextual process is based on struggle, on hostility among texts, and on the ultimate death of some as others are given new life.

A comparison between Goytisolo and Jorge Luis Borges, who for some is the Hispanic practitioner of intertextuality par excellence, reveals the basic difference between the structuralist understanding of the term and Goytisolo's. In Borges's "Pierre Menard, autor del *Quijote*," there is a playful superimposition of an invented text, Pierre Menard's, onto the real text by Cervantes. The interplay, the dialogue between texts, results in a subversion of the original form of each including that of Borges himself, for when the narrator cites Menard's *Quijote* in order to show the difference between the two texts, he does not change a single comma from Cervantes's original.[10] Borges tells us, as does Kristeva, that texts take on new significations when placed in conjunction with others, when lifted from one and inserted into another. Goytisolo's imitation of Larra, on the other hand, involves an active ideological struggle: Goytisolo and Larra versus the Hispanic tradition. In Goytisolo's work, there is an alienated real world that sets the linguistic battle into motion. The search for language, the attempt to uncover the sources of linguistic expression, is not self-sufficient. Alienation, authenticity, and history (social and literary) are still for Goytisolo very real forces that, in some instances, seem to transcend language itself. Goytisolo's intertextual endeavor is demonstrative of one of the crucial dilemmas of the modern age: the conflict between the existentialist stance in which all life is perceived and arranged through the eyes of an estranged subject and the structuralist view in which the world exists as a series of conventions independent of a perceiving subject. Ironically, while Goytisolo pays a great deal of lip service to the structuralist view, his mode of writing is an arena of existential confusion, conflict, and turmoil.

3. *Señas de identidad:*
The Intertextual Subversion Begins

The first phase of Goytisolo's new trilogy marks his break with his early mode of writing, a transformation that initiates an aggressive and violent process of textual contamination. The personal and ideological circumstances surrounding the change in Goytisolo have led to the ultimate alteration in his mode of writing, to the voice with which he feels most comfortable today. The personal shift is evidenced in one of the most provocative and penetrating interviews with the author to date: the one by Emir Rodríguez Monegal that took place almost immediately after the publication of *Señas*.[1] Unlike most interviews, which are chiefly ceremonies designed to heighten an author's reputation, the Goytisolo–Rodríguez Monegal exchange reflects the intricate self-examination and self-criticism that Goytisolo had undergone from 1963 to 1966, before and during the writing of the first volume of the second trilogy.

In that interview, he expresses his disdain for the novels written before the travelogues and says that describing social misery and oppression from a third-person point of view is a mark of literary dishonesty. This third-person omniscient narrator is for Goytisolo little short of a god, an entity that dominates all the characters, telling them what to do and how to think. If the author proposes to describe the reality of Spanish society, says Goytisolo, he must understand that his is only one view of that reality (p. 50). Thus the switch in Goytisolo's writing from third- to first-person narration is a conscious, even ideological, decision. *Campos de Níjar* is the only novel that, in Goytisolo's mind, is free from this hypocritical or falsely objective mode of writing, for it is an account of an actual trip taken by the author. *Señas* employs the first person and contains many autobiographical elements, but it is also the first novel built on an intricate relationship between protagonist and author, a relationship that manifests itself in the use of the second-person narrator. In the interview, Rodríguez Monegal affirms that the use of the *tú* involves not only a dialogue between the external Alvaro Mendiola and his inner conscience but also an exchange between the protagonist and the author (p. 54). The second person gives way to a dialogue in which the author may sit in judgment of the character he has created; it is the link between the Goytisolo of flesh and bone and the creation of a fictitious individual in his own image. Goytisolo agrees with Rodríguez Monegal when he states that the second person allows the author to intervene in the development of the character. The second-person point of view permits the author to laud or chastise the character and, for Goytisolo, it is a more impassioned form of writing than a narration in the first or third person would be (p. 54).

The interview further suggests that, in addition to being the vehicle for an inner dialogue that manifests a moral, existential, and cultural dilemma, the second-person narrator allows a written exchange between texts by the same author—in this case, Goytisolo. The Alvaro of *Señas* is a photographer who is in the process of making a documentary film on Franco's Spain. The motivating force for the documentary is Alvaro's estrangement from the culture and the homeland that have shaped his identity and at the same time have caused deep inner turmoil. Alvaro is in effect the Goytisolo who writes travelogues on Andalucía, the exiled Spaniard who cannot rid himself of his own culture. This relationship creates an interplay between the text that is being written and the texts that Goytisolo wrote before *Señas*, especially the documentary accounts of his travels through the south of Spain. The *tú* is indicative of a dialogue between writers and, therefore, between texts.

Related to this textual dialogue is another facet of Goytisolo's harsh assessment of his early works. In the interview, he points out that one of his greatest problems in the past was the lack of understanding of a literary tradition. Goytisolo declares that when he reads these early novels, he becomes irritated. To him, they are incomplete. They merely scrape the surface of interesting human problems, and, more important, they reflect a poor assimilation of other literature (p. 45). This statement may be interpreted as a commentary on the lack of intertextuality and on his uncritical use of other texts in the early novels (p. 45): "Se advierte en ellas una serie de lecturas no digeridas aún" ("One may detect in these works a series of undigested readings"). The writing of *Señas* marks the beginning of an attempt to assimilate other literature as the ensuing dialogue between texts becomes the unifying element of the trilogy. Goytisolo suggests the direction that his future writing will take when he discusses the sterilization of the Spanish language by worshipers of the Real Academia Española:

> los españoles hablamos de una forma muy tradicional, de una forma muy codificada. La cantidad de frases hechas y refranes que empleamos es enorme. Trasladado esto a la escritura de esa prosa supercastiza que tanto gusta a los lectores del ABC, ¡qué hipérboles! ¡qué metáforas!, ¡qué adjetivación! Y sobre todo, ¡qué tópicos! Séneca, el toro, Castilla, el Cid, el 98, Soria pura, me duele España. Los andaluces con sus nardos y jazmines y los castellanos con sus chopos. Algo repugnante. El escritor, cuando quiere romper con esta tradición, no se puede apoyar en una corriente lingüística popular; tiene que hacer un acto de violación individual, lo cual es mucho más difícil. Por eso . . . tengo que hacer una operación solitaria, una traición personal, una violación propia. (p. 48)

> (We Spaniards speak in a highly codified and traditional manner. The quantity of set phrases, proverbs, and clichés is enormous. These become transcribed into that excessively Castilian rhetorical prose that so pleases the readers of *ABC*. What hyperbole! What metaphors! What adjectives! And above all, what elevated subject matter: Seneca, bulls, Castile, the Cid, the Generation of '98, Soria the pure, the pains of Spain. The Andalusians with their flowers and jasmine and the Castilians with their poplar trees. It's repugnant. The writer who wishes to break with this tradition cannot rely on a current of popular language, he must engage in an individual act of treason, which is far more difficult. This is why I must commit a personal treason, an individual violation.)

Although these words are perfectly appropriate to *Don Julián*, they show a conscious wish to subvert a body of texts, a subversion that is only initiated in *Señas*. The first volume of the trilogy is Goytisolo's "beginning,"[2] for it unveils a heightened consciousness that works itself out in his subsequent novels.

It is evident that Goytisolo wanted his readers and critics to know that he had undergone personal and stylistic changes. But is the new Goytisolo genuine? Is Kessel Schwartz right when he asserts that Goytisolo has taken no significant new directions from 1954 to this day?[3] As far as personal considerations are concerned, only Goytisolo's psychiatrist can shed light on the matter. His writing, however, is another issue. There is no question that it has changed, and the point at which it does so is precisely where Goytisolo says it does: *Señas de identidad*.

The characteristics of Goytisolo's new mode of writing are best pinpointed by using Emile Benveniste's distinction between history and discourse. Goytisolo's espousal of Benvenistian theories may reveal another example of poorly digested theory, yet in this case, Benveniste is a good indicator. [4] According to Benveniste, history and discourse are two "planes of utterance," and each has distinguishing characteristics. The historical utterance necessitates the past tense as well as the third person and is limited to the narration of events. Benveniste shows through two examples of historical writing (a history of Greece and a passage from Balzac) that both the number and the nature of the tenses remain the same: "There is no need for them to change . . . and furthermore, there is no reason for the narration to come to a standstill since we can imagine the whole past of the world as one continuous narration" (p. 208). Discourse, on the other hand, is not limited to one person or tense because it assumes the presence of both speaker and listener: "It is primarily every variety of oral discourse of every nature and every level, from trivial conversation to the most elaborate oration. But it is also the mass of writing that reproduces oral discourse or that borrows its manner of expression and its purposes: correspondence, memoirs, plays, didactic works, in short, all the genres in which someone organizes what he says in the category of person" (p. 209). Employing all the personal forms as well as the widest variety of tenses, discourse appears in many types of language, even in historical narration (for example, the dialogue in a story). In Goytisolo's *Señas* there are many instances of pure discourse along with episodes presented as historical narratives. It is this interplay, this dialogue between two forms of writing, that signals the uniqueness of Goytisolo's new novel.

In a celebrated essay, "To Write: Intransitive Verb," Roland Barthes, who also had an impact on Goytisolo, applies several of the principles of Benvenistian linguistics in an attempt to describe the new techniques of modern literature.[5] Barthes discusses certain linguistic categories (temporality and person) and their relation to contemporary fiction. Linguistic time, as we have seen, is not the same in history as in discourse. The difference in time (the predominance of the present and future tenses in discourse as opposed to their absence in history) is related to the difference between person (the *I* and the *you*) and nonperson (the *he* or *it*). Both person and nonperson are apparent in discourse, but they differ in that "the non-person can never reflect the instance of discourse";[6] in other words, it can never reflect the moment or locality at which the utterance takes place. The intense immediacy created by discourse in a novel is, according to Barthes, an essential characteristic of Marcel Proust's writing and of much contemporary fiction. Goytisolo is no exception, and *Señas* provides examples of this new mode of writing interspersed with Benveniste's concept of historical narration.

Goytisolo's "history" revolves around the story of Alvaro Mendiola from his childhood to the present, as well as several interpolated sequences involving the re-creation of events in Spanish history. In one such case, the reader witnesses social upheaval in Yeste, a town in Andalucía. As the people gather to protest the mistreatment of prisoners by the civil guard, the narrator relates:

> Los vecinos de La Graya enviaron emisarios al alcalde de Yeste, al presidente y miembros de la Gestora, a los habitantes de las pedanías cercanas. Todos habían pasado la noche al sereno iluminados por el albedo de la luna, al acecho de los movimientos y voces de los civiles atrincherados en la casa-cuartel. Por caminos y trochas serranos,

orientándose por las estrellas, pineros, campesinos, carboneros, leñadores convergían puntualmente en su auxilio. La región entera velaba de pie. (p. 137)

(The people of La Graya sent emissaries to the mayor of Yeste, to the president and members of the Agency, to the inhabitants of the nearby communities. All had spent the night on watch, by the reflected light of the moon, spying on the movements and voices of the Civil Guards barricaded in the barracks. Along mountain roads and paths, guiding themselves by the stars, loggers, peasants, charcoal burners, woodcutters converged punctually to give help. The whole region was on foot and on guard.) (p. 114)

As in any historical narration, an omniscient storyteller describes the events in the third person. This feature of *Señas* is a carry-over from Goytisolo's early writing; the third-person narrator dominates the point of view in all the early novels from *Juegos de manos* to the last volume of *El pasado efímero*.

There are specific intertextual elements in *Señas* that also continue in the vein of the early novels. Certain characters in *Señas*, such as Professor Ayuso, are reminiscent of the omniscient liberal crusader of the youthful works. Professor Ayuso, like Giner, is a re-creation of a historical entity and is recognized not only as a unique individual within the plot of *Señas* but also as the embodiment of a tradition of frustrated Spanish liberalism. As Alvaro gazes at Ayuso's gravestone, the narrator lauds the intellectual:

Ayuso ha vivido con dignidad años difíciles, destierro, cárcel, persecuciones, ostracismo, olvido voluntario, armado con la única verdad de su palabra, sin claudicar jamás en el combate todo para acabar así, cubierto de tierra, cemento y ladrillo bajo la custodia de ellos, cuerpo indefenso al fin, definitivamente entre sus manos. (p. 105)

(Ayuso has lived through difficult years with dignity, exile, jail, persecution, ostracism, voluntary forgetfulness, armed only with the truth of his words, never backing down in the struggle, and it all ended like this, covered with earth, cement, and bricks, in their custody, a defenseless body at last, in their hands once and for all.) (p. 87)

In other instances the characters discuss and appraise specific figures and organizations from the civil war: Companys, Queipo de Llano, the anarchist and socialist political parties and trade unions such as the FAI, the CNT, and the UGT.

Yet all these examples do not explain Goytisolo's novelistic enterprise unless they are placed in the context of the totality of the book. The instances of historical narration are flashbacks, reminiscences of the protagonist's past experiences. Throughout *Señas* there is a dialogue between the past and the present as there is between the two forms of writing, history and discourse. More weight, however, is given to the latter, for the frame of this dialogue is always the present. Even the renditions of the past are situated within a discourse and seem to speak as separate entities, as discrete signs of Alvaro's identity. In many ways, the historical narration is a series of texts that make up what Alvaro has become, texts that Goytisolo interpolates within the broader context of Alvaro's present character. These texts personify not only Alvaro Mendiola but also the novelistic technique of Juan Goytisolo.

Intertextual Elements of Señas de identidad

The presence of outside texts in *Señas* operates on several levels. First, there are characters whose novelistic function depends on their reading of literature, philosophy, and newspapers, or on their perception of photographs and paintings. Second, Goytisolo juxtaposes a variety of texts against his own in order to create a conflict between two voices: that of the outside text and that of the main text. In these cases, Goytisolo interpolates the previous text within the main text. Third, Goytisolo changes the outside text in an attempt to contaminate and subvert its original signification.[7]

A central motif in *Señas* is the photograph, which embodies the snatches, bits, and pieces of Alvaro's life that are constantly being arranged and rearranged. As these photos evoke the memories of Alvaro's past, the reader is able to embrace a multitude of events, people, and situations that define what Alvaro has become. Memories of childhood and adolescence, the civil war, leftist student activity, experiences in Paris, and a return visit to Spain are all sparked by photographs. While these reproductions of Alvaro's life appear most frequently, other texts also encompass parts of the protagonist's identity: films, paintings, music (the constant, haunting sound of Mozart's *Requiem*), and, most important, literature. One of the most prevalent literary devices is the citation of a text as a tool in the development of a character. As Alvaro reconstructs his genealogy, he tries to recall the various members of his family who had an influence on him. He remembers, for example, that his uncle César was a "lector admirativo del *Mein Kampf* "(p. 36) and that another relative, his uncle Eulogio, was similarly a "lector concienzudo de Spengler y de Keyserling" (p. 413). The mention of these texts and writers places both relatives on Alvaro's (and Goytisolo's) "wrong" side; they manifest the aspect of Alvaro's family background that represents power, money, and worn-out values, an aspect that, unfortunately for Alvaro, is far more pervasive than the liberal side. The more tolerant and politically progressive part of Alvaro is represented by his great-uncle Néstor, who is (p. 56) "idolatrado por tu [second-person narrator] abuela y silenciado por el resto de los tuyos" ("idolatrized by your maternal grandmother and kept in silence by the rest of your relatives," p. 45). It is significant that copies of texts by Charles Baudelaire, Paul Verlaine, Clarín [Leopoldo Alas], and Mariano José de Larra are found in Néstor's library. The narrator states (p. 56) that these texts "debían alimentar más tarde tu inconformismo" ("would later on feed your non-conformism," p. 45). The implication behind the use of this device is clear: tell me what you read, and I'll show you who you are.[8]

The reading of texts is of central importance to the protagonist's development. In one of the most vivid scenes in the work, the narrator recalls a time during the civil war when Alvaro (then a child) and Señorita Lourdes, his nanny, witnessed the burning of a church. Although much of what happens revolves around Barcelona at the height of wartime activity, the actual setting for this scene is a library. While at the library, Alvaro remembers how

Lourdes instilled extreme feelings of religious piety in him through the telling and retelling of stories from the Bible and from the lives of saints. Alvaro recalls one particular time when he zealously sought a book that Lourdes had read to him. Among all the books with high-sounding religious titles—*Las virtudes y los vicios (Virtues and Vices), La reina del cielo (The Queen of Heaven), La devoción de San José (The Devotions of Saint Joseph), El verdadero siervo de la Virgen Santísima (The True Servant of the Blessed Virgin)*—he cannot find the one he is looking for, *Historias de niños mártires (Stories of Child Martyrs)*, and has to settle for *Vidas de niños santos (Lives of Child Saints)*. Alvaro notices that there is a similarity between the writing style of the book and the tone of Lourdes's speech. In a flashback, she tells him stories of martyred saints, and as her words merge with the words of the book, she reads to her pupil:

> —Oye bien, que la historia no ha concluido. . . . Obstinado el prefecto quiso satisfacer su diabólica sed de venganza ordenando que la Santa fuese ligada a un aspa de madera y que su cuerpo fuese materialmente asado con hachones encendidos. En el instante en que rindió su alma a Dios se vio salir de su boca una paloma blanquísima que volaba hacia el cielo, símbolo de su espíritu virginal que subía a recibir la corona del martirio. . . . ¿Estás llorando, hijo mío? (p. 22)

> ("Listen carefully, the story isn't over. . . . 'The headstrong Prefect, in an attempt to satisfy his diabolical thirst for vengeance, ordered the Saint tied to a wooden cross and her body roasted with flaming torches. At the moment she gave up her soul to God there was seen to fly out of her mouth a pure white dove which ascended to heaven, the symbol of her virginal spirit which was going up to receive its martyr's crown.' . . . Are you crying, child?") (p. 16)

Goytisolo is not engaged in the creation of an imaginary text but rather in the re-creation of a specific document that he has revealed as the source of his attack. One of the many books that he claims had inspired *Señas* is a collection of stories of martyred saints, a passage from which reads: "mandaron que fuese Eulalia fuertemente atada a un palo, o bien a un aspa de madera y que su cuerpo fuese materialmente asado con hechones encendidos . . . En el momento en que exhaló el último suspiro, se vió salir de su boca una paloma blanquísima que volaba hacia el Cielo, símbolo de su alma virginal que subía a recibir la corona del martirio" ("They ordered Eulalia firmly tied to a stake or a wooden cross and her body roasted with flaming torches. . . . The moment she breathed her last breath, there was seen to fly out of her mouth a pure white dove that ascended to heaven, the symbol of her virginal spirit that was going up to receive its martyr's crown").[9]

These stories reappear in the novel with such frequency that the protagonist begins to confuse the reality of the texts with the reality of life. As the city becomes an arena of conflict among republicans, anarchists, socialists, and fascists, Alvaro and Lourdes turn into objects of ridicule. Alvarito follows his nanny to the only seemingly safe place left in the city—a church—but when they arrive they find that the church is burning. They are prevented from going any further by two anarchist soldiers. Lourdes, however, remains persistent and tries to push her way through, mouthing her sacred words (p. 30), " 'Pasión de Cristo, confórtame . . . Oh buen Señor, óyeme' " (" 'Passion of Christ, comfort me . . . Oh, hear me, good Jesus,' " p. 23). Alvarito is also convinced of his own righteousness (p. 26): " 'No tengo miedo a la muerte, señorita Lourdes' " (" 'I'm not afraid to die, Señorita Lourdes,' " p. 19). It is clear, however, that their martyrdom is prescribed, for the narrator assures us that Alvarito's preceding statement was (p. 26) "una frase aprendida del libro" ("a sentence learned from a book," p. 19).

The development of a character through the citation of the works that he or she reads is not uncommon in literature. Allusions to other works and figures are often elements of a conflict between literature and life, a tension that contributes to the development of the eternal theme of illusion versus reality. The nineteenth-century European novel, for example, makes use of the theme frequently. In Clarín's *La regenta* Ana Ozores reads the life of Santa Teresa in much the same way as Flaubert's Emma, the protagonist of *Madame Bovary*, reads religious works during her short-lived period of zealous piety. Yet the episode in *Señas* that describes the relationship between Lourdes and

Alvarito is more than a renewed expression of an old literary theme. It is evident that the citations of the religious works are used as aids in character portrayal, yet there is also a linguistic relationship between the main text and the cited text that is not as distinct in novels such as *La regenta* and *Madame Bovary*. In those nineteenth-century texts the authors use certain themes from other works to develop their characters. Ana's husband Víctor, in *La regenta,* reads the Spanish cloak-and-dagger plays and incorporates them into his life. By the same token, Flaubert's citation of the texts "devoured" by Emma is a manifestation of the protagonist's inability to distinguish between literature and life. Goytisolo, however, uses the words of these outside texts as well as their titles. He takes great care to point out the concrete relationship between the texts as he stresses the merger between Lourdes's speech and the religious works (p. 21): "De vuelta al campo habías examinado el libro, redactado aproximadamente en el mismo lenguaje que el de la señorita Lourdes y el pasado había irrumpido en ti de modo imprevisto, metamorfoseando tu libro en el perdido libro, tu voz en la atiplada voz de la señorita de compañía" ("On your way back to the country you had examined the book, written in approximately the same language as Señorita Lourdes's, and the past had erupted in you in an unforeseen way, turning your book into the lost book, your voice into the flutey voice of the nursemaid," p. 15). The new book and the old one fuse, and together they mesh with the voice of Señorita Lourdes as well as with that of Alvaro himself. The descriptions of the martyred saints and the suffering of the Virgin Mary appear in a form that takes on a dual shape. The citation from the religious work is both a dialogue (Lourdes's moral lesson for Alvarito) and a transcription of a religious text into the body of the work.

At one point in the depiction of the influence of Lourdes on Alvarito, Goytisolo places his adult protagonist, Alvaro, in front of a mirror and has him recall the words of a religious text. Alvaro's memory of his ingenuous boyhood attempt to imitate the martyrs engenders the recollection of the voice of Señorita

Lourdes (p. 23): "arrullado por la gozosa voz de la Señorita Lourdes que, gafas caladas sobre la nariz, parecía espiar siempre, con astucia, las emociones pintadas en tu rostro" ("lulled by the pleasant voice of Señorita Lourdes who, with her glasses lowered on her nose, always seemed to be astutely spying at the emotions painted on your face," p. 17). This description immediately precedes a specific quotation from the religious work, which again is the voice of Lourdes (p. 23): " 'Distinguióse bien pronto la pequeña por su piedad y buen corazón' " (" 'The little girl was known for her piety and good heart at an early age,' " p. 17). Alvarito and Lourdes deceive themselves through books as do Emma Bovary and Ana Ozores, yet in Goytisolo this self-deception is a manifestation of the power of words, a very real and intense power that overwhelms life itself. It seems strange that Alvaro (the young adult) can remember with such precision the words and expressions from religious texts that were read to him as a child, but his precise recollection is not peculiar when placed in the context of Goytisolo's conception of the power of language. At certain points in *Señas*, language creates reality; to remember an incident in childhood is to remember the language of that incident. The reality of Alvaro's indentity and the reality of Spanish history (the civil war and its effects) take shape through the language of that history and through the language of Alvaro's past.

The increasing importance attached to language becomes apparent in the linguistic manipulation between texts, which is implicit in the appendixes of *La Chanca* and explicit in *Señas*. Intertexts are immersed within the main body of *Señas*'s text, clearly exposing a conflict between the two. In *Señas* an important device in the development of the events surrounding the arrest and imprisonment of Alvaro's friend Antonio is the "surveillance record" taken directly from actual police notes concerning a subversive political group (SCML). This police log appears as italicized segments that Goytisolo has distributed throughout the fourth chapter (pp. 159–237), among other sections dealing with the leftist students with whom Alvaro associates. At the beginning of the chapter, Goytisolo sets the tone for his manipulation of the two separate but related lines of narration.

El diario de vigilancias de la Brigada Regional de Investigación Social (confiado a Antonio por su abogado defensor después del proceso), expedientes y actas del Juzgado de Instrucción que viera la causa, asociaciones de ideas y recuerdos no filtrados aún por el severo tamiz de la memoria (pertenecientes a épocas distintas, sin ningún denominador común) interpolaban de modo caótico el relato de Antonio sobre su detención y confinamiento (rehecho luego por ti con ayuda de Dolores). Sometida a los cánones imperiosos de lo real tu imaginación se resarcía componiendo con morosidad las situaciones, limando las aristas del diálogo, atando cabos y rellenando huecos, manejando con soltura su influjo catalizador. (p. 160)

(The surveillance record of the Regional Social Investigation Brigade (given to Antonio by his defense lawyer after the trial), the transcript and records of the Arraignment Court that had heard the case, the associations of ideas and memories that had not yet been filtered through the demanding sieve of memory (belonging to different periods, with no common denominator) interpolated in a chaotic way Antonio's story of his arrest and imprisonment (all put together again later on by you with Dolores's help). Submitting to the demanding canons of reality, your imagination compensated for it by slowly putting situations together, polishing the edges of dialogues, tying up loose ends and filling holes, skillfully manipulating its effect as a catalyst.) (p. 134)

The effect of the interpolation of these segments is unlike the linguistic fusion between Alvarito's religious stories and the voice of Señorita Lourdes. In this case, there is a diametric contrast, a struggle between two positions that are hostile to one another. The language of the police evidences an intense concern (almost an obsession) with objectivity. Goytisolo pinpoints every minute detail of the activities of this subversive group—the hour at which they leave their homes; the bars they frequent; every acquaintance, no matter how insignificant; their past involvement in political activity, including their party affiliations during the war (p. 168): *"Domingo, día 3—A las 8'45 salen Gorila y Gitano de casa de éste y se trasladan en autobús al final de la calle Mallorca"* (*"Sun., Nov. 3—At 8:45 A.M. Gorilla and Gypsy leave latter's house and take bus to end of Calle Mallorca,"* p. 141). This

objectivity and apparent impartiality stand in contrast to other
segments in which impressions of the situations and events are
tainted with opinions (p. 195): "La conversación seguía el cauce
de siempre: eran las mismas voces, las mismas palabras, la misma
expresión amarga de una existencia frustrada e inútil" ("The
conversation followed the usual course: there were the same
voices, the same words, the same bitter expression of a frustrated
and useless existence," p. 163). Yet underlying the "unbiased"
nature of the official language is the presence of an assumed truth,
the righteousness of the authorities' desire to liquidate the
opposition. At one point (p. 179), the civil war is called "nuestra
Cruzada" ("our crusade"), a term common in the official language
but unquestionably biased. The narrator confronts this falsely
scientific tone with his own view of the role of the police
throughout Spanish history (p. 229): "Sobre eso no cabía la
menor duda: la policía funcionaba perfectamente. Cinco siglos de
vigilancia, inquisición y censura habían configurado poco a poco
la estructura moral de este organismo único, considerado incluso
por enemigos y detractores como faro y modelo de las múltiples
instituciones sanitarias que, inspirándose en él, proliferan hoy por
el mundo" ("There was not the slightest doubt about it: the police
had worked perfectly. Five centuries of vigilance, inquisition, and
censorship had slowly configured the moral structure of this
unique organism, considered by its enemies and detractors as a
beacon and model of the many sanitary institutions that, taking
their inspiration from it, are proliferating throughout the world,"
p. 190). The hostility between texts is not the consequence of
manipulation by the author. Goytisolo does not create both sides
of the coin as would the arbiter of a fair contest. He inserts a real
text taken from an actual criminal proceeding and places his own
text in opposition to it. In his own words, the police diary serves
him as concrete material against which he can struggle: he says in
a note (SCML) that in *Señas* he assumes the role of a painter who
encrusts a particular object onto his painting instead of portraying
or reproducing that object.

The insertion of unaltered texts in *Señas* takes many other forms. Alvaro's urge to re-create his past is based on memories of experiences spawned by the recollections of specific objects, many of which are texts. The language of these texts assumes an autonomous role outside Goytisolo's novel. They have, or had at one time, their own purpose, their own reason for having been written. But placed within *Señas*, they take on new life and become dependent on another text for their signification. These intertexts, further signs of Alvaro's identity, continually reappear throughout the work. They are Goytisolo's tools in the re-creation of Alvaro's past. The protagonist relives his childhood with the aid of postcards, photos, prints, and knickknacks that have special significance to his life. At times the captions of these pictures are "encrusted" onto the text of *Señas* as they become intertexts. Perhaps the most intensely personal of all these objects from the past is a letter from a Cuban slave, mistress to one of Alvaro's ancestors who made his fortune in Cuba when it was still a Spanish colony. Although the words of the letter were deleted from the second edition of *Señas*, their impact is felt throughout the entire novel as well as through the whole of the trilogy.[10] The letter is another sign of the tension in Alvaro's life that causes an irresolvable conflict between his two selves—the Alvaro who is a product of Spanish history and culture, and the Alvaro who is morally and socially repelled by that culture (pp. 13–14): "prisionero de un personaje que no eras tú" ("prisoner of a character who was not you," p. 9).

The integration of unaltered texts throughout *Señas* is reminiscent of the textual interpolations found in the travelogues. The presence of these texts is a further manifestation of Goytisolo's abandonment of the realism of *Juegos, Duelo,* and *El pasado efímero.* The attempt to reflect social reality is rejected in favor of a transcription of that reality. Goytisolo gathers the texts that he needs and inserts them into strategic places within his own text: obituaries (p. 123), the program of festivities for the holidays of Yeste (pp. 126–27), a poem from a magazine (p. 258), the sign on a building (p. 319), the diary of a Catalan worker (pp. 375–95), and a tourist guide (pp. 399–402). The worker's diary

is an important example, for it reveals the changing nature of
Goytisolo's social criticism. The diary appears in separate pieces
interspersed among accounts of trips taken by the protagonist to
his native land and back to Paris. The diary is a document as is the
police log, but in the case of the diary, the reader sympathizes
with the plight of those who were abused for political reasons
immediately after the civil war, especially those in dire economic
need. The transcription of the diary is free from the assessment
and manipulation of an omniscient narrator; it speaks for itself (p.
376): "y esta silla y este cesto saben que cuanto digo es verdad
verdadera pues ellos recuerdan los golpes que me dieron con la
fusta y el poco pan que mi mujer recogía por las casas y al cabo
de un año me pasaron de la cárcel al hospital y de allí me
soltaron con un papel que decía José Bernabeu ha estado preso
por rojo" ("and this chair and this basket know that everything
Im [*sic*] saying is the real truth because they remember when they
whipped me and the small amount of bread my wife would get
from house to house and after a year they transferred me from the
jail to the hospital and from there they released me with a piece of
paper that said José Bernabeu had been arrested for being a
Red," p. 312).[11] In the interpolation of these words, Goytisolo
assumes the role of a reader, one who sees poetry (the personification of the chair and the basket) in the description of a common
worker.

   Distinct from the direct "encrustation" or interpolation of
unaltered outside texts are many instances in which Goytisolo
manipulates and changes the previous text for his own purposes.
In the former cases, we witness the clash between two separate
and diametrically opposed texts; in the latter, this conflict is found
within one text. The result is a subversion of the previous text, a
corruption of its original intentions. This form of linguistic
manipulation manifests itself in the segments that appear as
quotations that describe Alvaro's moral deficiencies. Goytisolo
takes these segments directly from articles in prominent Spanish
newspapers *(El Espectador, La Vanguardia, Pueblo)* that evaluate
his own contribution to the contemporary Spanish literary scene.

In order to fully apprehend the function of these segments, it is important to understand the polemical context from which they issue. In the early sixties, two political incidents that had direct effects on Goytisolo sparked a polemic that continued well into the decade (from about 1960 to 1968). [12] In February 1960, Goytisolo's brother Luis, also a writer, was arbitrarily arrested and held without charge for several months. This act spurred a concerted campaign of protest among French, Italian, Latin American, and Spanish intellectuals. In a separate incident that occurred in February 1961 in the Teatro del Corso in Milan, Italy, a smoke bomb exploded during the showing of *Notes sur l'émigration,* a documentary film based on Goytisolo's novel *La resaca.* No one was injured, but during the commotion the film was stolen. A week later, several articles in the Spanish press as well as broadcasts on Spanish radio and television described the film as Communist propaganda and linked it to terrorist activity directed toward the Spanish embassy in Geneva. It later became apparent that the film was stolen by avowed Italian fascists with the collaboration of the Spanish secret police. These incidents caused great furor and marked the beginning of a literary debate over the artistic quality of Goytisolo's novels. The Spanish literary establishment severely criticized all aspects of Goytisolo's writing, while his defenders (several prominent Spanish intellectuals) stressed, in letters to editors, the merits of his literary production.

The illuminating factor in the critical reviews is not the disapproval of Goytisolo's style (his allegedly improper and ungrammatical use of the language of the Real Academia Española) but the harsh assessment of his moral character. These *ad hominem* attacks, which appear in *Señas* as further marks of Alvaro's identity, are presented as monologues spoken by a first-person-plural narrator who is the "voice of official Spain," the mouthpiece of a country whose sacred mission is to spread the doctrine of righteousness. In these segments, Alvaro comes under severe criticism (p. 9): "Instalado en París cómodamente instalado en París ... con más costumbres francesas que españolas" ("Established in Paris comfortably established in Paris

. . . with more French habits than Spanish ones," p. 5). The reviews disclose the fact that Goytisolo's permanent residence in Paris is a cause of much hostility among the literary critics of the newspapers. In one of these journalistic pieces, Goytisolo is characterized as a young gigolo who occasionally resides in Paris (SCML), and in another as a writer whose long absences are evidence of his wish to evade Spanish reality through a comfortable nonconformity (SCML). In *Señas* the same moral appraisal appears (p. 9): "evadido de las realidades del momento en un fácil confortable y provechoso inconformismo" ("evading the realities of the moment with an easy comfortable and advantageous nonconformity," p. 5). It is ironic that these portrayals reveal as much about this *nosotros* ("we," the voice of Spain) as they do about Alvaro. The haughty and grandiose tone of the *nosotros* resounds as the speaker attempts to defend his nation against verbal foreign attacks:

> en nuestra patria a partir de la Contrarreforma para acá España viene padeciendo los ataques más injustos irritantes e intolerables que a nación alguna se le hayan podido dirigir ataques que de manera sistemática tienen su rebrote periódico desde la taimada trinchera de la mentira del resentimiento de la información malintencionada y tendenciosa de todo lo que implique atentar contra la soberana decisión de un país de gobernarse por sí mismo sin ingerencias foráneas ni arbitrarias imposiciones y si estos ataques son indignantes cuando nos viene de manos extranjera [*sic*] no merecen más que desprecio si proceden de un compatriota dispuesto a colocar la turbina en la cloaca con el propósito de convertirse en un personajillo al pairo de posiciones políticas que conocemos hasta la saciedad. (p. 10)

> (in our homeland since the Counter-Reformation up till the present Spain has suffered under the most unjust irritating and intolerable attacks that any nation could receive attacks which systematically and periodically emerge from the crafty hole of lies resentment ill-intentioned and tendentious information everything that implies an attack against the sovereign decision of a country to govern itself in its own way without outside interference or arbitrary impositions and if these attacks are irritating when they come from a foreign land they only deserve a sneer when they are the work of a fellow countryman ready to sink his turbine into the sewer with the idea of making himself a famous little person by aligning himself with political positions of which we have had our fill.) (p. 6).

This next passage comes directly from an article in *Pueblo:*

> Desde la Contrarreforma para acá, España viene padeciendo los ataques más injustos, más irritantes, más intolerables que a nación alguna se le hayan podido dirigir. Ataques que, de una manera sistemática, tienen su rebrote periódico desde la taimada trinchera de la mentira, del resentimiento, de la información malintencionada y tendenciosa, de todo lo que significa ir contra el derecho sagrado que un pueblo tiene de ser respetado en su verdad y en su esencia, de todo que significa atentar contra el soberano derecho que un pueblo civilizado tiene de gobernarse por sí mismo sin extrañas ingerencias ni arbitrarias imposiciones. (SCML)

> (Since the Counter-Reformation up until the present day, Spain has suffered the most unjust, irritating, and intolerable attacks that any nation could receive, attacks that systematically and periodically emerge from the crafty hole of lies, resentment, ill-intentioned and tendentious information, everything that is an attack on the sovereign right of a civilized nation to govern itself without alien and arbitrary intrusions and impositions.)

This indignant writer further points out that these attacks are intolerable when they are voiced by foreigners but unforgivable when expressed by a traitor.

In *Señas* Goytisolo continues this dualistic portrayal of Spain and Alvaro (p. 12): "sabemos que eres barcelonés pese al apellido asturiano pero asturiano o barcelonés suponiendo que Barcelona no te inspire emoción ni la tierra asturiana suscite deleite en tu alma danos a todos la espalda y mira hacia otros horizontes" ("we know that you are a Barcelonan in spite of your Asturian name but Asturian or Barcelonan supposing that Barcelona does not inspire any emotion in you or the land of Asturias raise any warm feeling in your soul turn your back on all of us and look toward other horizons," p. 8). In *La Vanguardia*, an irate columnist had addressed himself personally to Goytisolo in the form of an open letter: "We believe you are Catalan in spite of your Basque surname" (note the first person plural). He goes on to say, in the same words found in *Señas*, that if neither Catalonia nor the Basque country inspire Goytisolo, he should "look toward other horizons" (SCML): a Spanish version of "love it or leave it."

In these passages, a parodic devaluation or degradation begins that is carried to its full consequence in *Don Julián*. Goytisolo destroys the arrogance and archaic grandiloquence of these literary reviews and articles by infiltrating their style. The absence of punctuation and the manner in which the words and phrases overlap—"nuestros adversarios cualquiera que sea el Régimen que exista en nuestra patria que a partir de la Contrarreforma" (p. 10)—transform the articles (the previous texts) into a unified, monotonous voice that seems to go on indefinitely. These segments are of utmost importance to the novel, for they unveil the object of Alvaro's fury: the regime's archaic values and outmoded traditions. Yet these values are not easily rejected because they resound with the voices of Alvaro's past: the inner monitor of Alvaro's conscience, which tells him that he has strayed from what he should have done, and the exterior tone of Spanish society and history, the journalism that justifies the status quo.

These voices reveal a trace not only of Alvaro's past life but also of Goytisolo's past texts. The sound of the loudspeakers in *Fiestas* and *La resaca* (the speeches and the radio that interrupt Giner's discourse) continues in *Señas* in the form of these haunting defamations of Alvaro's character. The invectives uncover a trace of an issue that appears vividly in *Don Julián*—the mythification and demythification of official or sacred Spain. In *Señas* as well as in *El pasado efímero*, the spirit of this official Spain emerges through these mythological voices, the collective unconscious of a worn-out culture.

Alvaro's search for identity is parallel to Goytisolo's search for a meaningful voice through writing. The autobiographical nature of *Señas* is undeniable, yet the similarities between its author and its protagonist must be viewed not as a relationship between the life of a man and the life of a character but as a relationship between texts. The broad definition of *text* advanced by Kristeva and Barthes[13] converts Alvaro's search for authenticity through photographs, films, music, and newspaper clippings into a search for texts. In like manner, Goytisolo's reaction to Spanish censorship and his answer to the moral indictment directed toward him in the press become a search for texts, a search for a language with which he can express his authentic voice. Alvaro is the embodiment of Goytisolo's textual search.

The quest for texts, however, falls short in *Señas*. Neither Alvaro nor Goytisolo likes what he finds; their own identities are repugnant to them both. As Alvaro gazes over the city of Barcelona with the aid of the telescope reserved for tourists, he realizes that there is no reason to continue the search, for there is nothing in his culture worth holding on to. Toward the end of the novel, the voice of the *nosotros* is heard for the last time (p. 421):

> nuestra firmeza es inconmovible ningún esfuerzo tuyo
>   logrará socavarla
> piedra somos y piedra permaneceremos
> no te empecines más márchate fuera
> mira hacia otros horizontes danos a todos la espalda
> olvídate de nosotros y te olvidaremos
> tu pasión fue un error
> repáralo
> SALIDA
> SORTIE
> EXIT
> AUSGANG

> (our firmness is unmovable no effort of yours will be able
>   to undermine it
> we are stone and stone we will remain
> don't insist any more go away
> look toward other horizons turn your back on all of us
> forget about us and we will forget you
> your passion was a mistake
> heed it
> SALIDA
> SORTIE
> EXIT
> AUSGANG) (p. 351)

Goytisolo's continued use of other languages in the culminating words of the novel—"INTRODUZCA LA MONEDA ... GELDSTUCK EINWARFEN [*sic*]" (p. 422)—is evidence of an invasion of Alvaro's mother tongue. This linguistic invasion is not an alternative in *Señas*, for it represents the omnipresence of tourism, Spain's most lucrative national resource. Both protagonist and author remain defeated; in their search, they have found everything, and they have found nothing.

In the early works, the intertextual process begins with the use of Machado's poem and figures from Spanish history. The optimistic course of the poem is altered with an element of ambiguity, and the vociferation of a lost empire becomes a dissonant object of ridicule as Goytisolo's hostility toward his own culture grows. In *Fiestas* the loudspeaker overpowers the characters; in *La resaca* it promotes indifference and passivity. But in *Señas* the reader witnesses the commencement of an intricate process of devaluation, degradation, and subversion of official Spain.

The relationship between texts in *Señas* is more intricate than it is in the early novels. This work, Goytisolo's culminating narrative of civil-war and post-civil-war Spanish life, blends not merely one or two texts but a variety of texts, resulting in a multifaceted conflict within a single work. The increasingly violent intertextual struggles mirror Goytisolo's increasing aversion toward his own culture. There is no recourse for Alvaro's hatred because it is, in essence, a self-hatred. It is the impossible problem that he fails bitterly to resolve. Intertextuality in *Señas*, the mixture of different texts, remains subordinate to an existential problem, an all-encompassing issue that governs the structure of the work. The textual struggle is, in effect, a cultural and existential confrontation between the author and his world. But the trilogy of treason has not ended; Alvaro's problem will reopen. In the subsequent volumes of the trilogy textual manipulation becomes more and more intricate as the attempt to resolve the existential crisis through the subversion of Alvaro's (and Goytisolo's) mother tongue becomes a linguistic reconquest of Spain by Africa—the forces of corruption and contagion. From now on, all will be "destrucción, el fuego."[14]

4. *Reivindicación del Conde don Julián:* Assault on a Literary Tradition

The new conception of writing evidenced in the interplay between history and discourse in *Señas de identidad* arrives at its logical consequence in *Don Julián:* writing as pure discourse. In *Don Julián* historical writing is virtually nonexistent. The concept of the novel as pure discourse puts the notions of plot, story, and even character into question. The omniscient narrator, "the little god," as Goytisolo calls it in his interview with Rodríguez Monegal,[1] takes the form of first- and second-person pronouns whose time references are the present and the future. Commentary, monologue, and attempts to influence behavior all become the mainstays of *Don Julián.* The effect of this discourse is to focus the reader's attention on the use of language rather than on the presumed truth of historical narration. In Goytisolo's new linguistic manipulation, language refers to itself instead of to real objects.

Yet hidden behind this loss of reality in language, this rejection of history (in the Benvenistian sense), is a historical vision. *Don Julián* is a declaration of war against established values, customs, and myths. True, the war is a linguistic one that seeks to annihilate the texts that embody post-civil-war society as well as those that represent the totality of Spanish culture. But the assault against language is incomplete without the specific historical perspective that assumes the existence of real events, real figures, and real situations. This paradox—the conflict between a self-referential system of language and a strict analysis of Spanish history—dominates the second phase of Goytisolo's trilogy, and the self-exiled Spaniard does all that he can to resolve the contradiction. For Goytisolo, Spain's historically characteristic obsession with national and religious righteousness (the reconquest, the Inquisition, the discovery and usurpation of the New World, the insistence on monarchy as the most virtuous form of government, the civil war) is built on the rejection, denial, and liquidation of the Judaic and especially the Arabic influences on Spanish culture. In *Don Julián*, the paradigm of Goytisolo's new view of his native land, the author goes back to the moment when the Arabs entered Spain from the coast of what is now Morocco and extended the northern border of the African continent into Europe. He chooses this crucial moment not only for its penetrating impact on Spanish history but also for its historical vagueness. Little is known of Conde don Julián, the man who is alleged to have opened the doors of Spain to the Moors. For a concrete picture of him, we must turn to the written accounts of the Arab conquest, most of which remain in the category of literature: the *Visigothic Chronicles*, the *Poem of Fernán González*, Alfonso el Sabio's *Crónica general (General Chronicle)*, the *Romancero (The Romances of the King Don Rodrigo)*, and virtually all the texts in which Don Julián appears either as a historical figure or as a fictional character. For this reason the topic of Goytisolo's discourse is not Spain itself, its history, or its present social conditions. Instead, his objects of commentary are the written versions of that history. Goytisolo places his discourse *(Don Julián)* within a context of Spanish historiography.

The writing of history is an extremely important aspect of *Don Julián* and is intricately connected to the intertextual process of linguistic subversion. *Don Julián* is not an objective assessment of various perspectives on the history of Spain, for Goytisolo takes sides. In the polemic created by the writings of Américo Castro on the origin of Spain and on the peculiarities of the Iberian peninsula, Goytisolo affirms his allegiance to those intellectuals who are in agreement with Castro. Goytisolo considers Castro one of the few objective and enlightened voices in Spanish historiography. He incorporates many of Castro's arguments into *Don Julián*, while he degrades and ridicules those figures and events in Spanish history that Castro believes are mythical.[2] Castro's works become central intertexts in the second volume of the trilogy; his essays and historical investigations are allies in Julián's wholehearted attempt at "demythification."

Castro appears in *Don Julián* only twice, in an epigraph to the second chapter (p. 89) and in the concluding "Advertencia" (p. 241), but the historian's presence is felt on nearly every page. Castro is for Goytisolo another heterodox Spaniard, one who, like José María Blanco White, Mariano José de Larra, and Luis Cernuda,[3] stands in contrast to what is considered the mainstream of Spanish intellectual history. Castro's dissenting vision of Spain is built on the crucial concept of the *morada vital*, or the collective consciousness of a society or cultural group. In this view, individuals of a society are not the passive recipients of determined political and economic forces but the creators of their own history. Human beings invent themselves and construct their own style of life and identity. In effect, they create their own concept of "we," the identity that defines their social behavior. These ideas are of vital importance in the apprehension of Castro's view of the cultural idiosyncrasies of the Iberian peninsula, for, according to Castro, the structure of Spanish history is based on them. For the historian, Spain became a nation the moment that Moorish warriors crossed the Mediterranean, a historical event that created a vital bond between what was then a Visigothic monarchy and Africa. The threat to the inhabitants of Hispania was not so much political as it was religious. To fend off the attack of Islam, Christianity needed to strengthen itself by a renewed affirmation of religious truth. The Visigoths became Spaniards when they forged a new group identity, the Spanish *morada vital*, as a result of this religious threat. This *morada vital* created the tripartite caste system on which Castro has insisted in virtually all his work since *España en su historia (Spain in Its History)*.[4] For Castro, the interrelationships and conflicts among these three castes— Christians, Jews, and Muslims—are the key to the structure of Spanish history. Further, the intransigence of the ruling Christian caste and its phobia for any contradictory or nonconforming elements are, in effect, the cause of Spain's backwardness in comparison to other countries.

Goytisolo shares the basic tenets of Castro's severe and pessimistic view of Spanish history and culture. In its depiction of Spain in general and in specific scenes that restate Castro's argument about certain facets of Spanish history, *Don Julián* is a testimonial to Goytisolo's reverence for the erudite Spanish historian. Goytisolo's re-creation of the character of Don Julián lends itself perfectly to the restatement of Castro's arguments, for one finds in the count of Ceuta the roots, the source, of subsequent historical events and, more important, the core of the Spanish *morada vital*. Conde don Julián represents a peculiarly Spanish original sin. In *La realidad histórica (The Historical Reality)*, Castro remarks on Don Julián's impact not only on Spanish literature but also on the Spanish soul. He writes that the Count Julian legend is second only to that of Saint James in its impact on the Spanish consciousness: the story fomented the most profound feelings of historical and cultural pride in all Spaniards and actually became an integral part of Spanish history (pp. 318–19). Goytisolo renders Don Julián a living figure who embodies virtually all of Spanish history, culture, and politics.

As Goytisolo's re-creation of Conde don Julián is a living expression of Castro's historical posture, specific motifs in the novel are also reminiscent of Castro's views. The constant presence of Seneca in *Don Julián* is typical. In one of the subchapters of *La realidad histórica* titled "Séneca no era español, ni los españoles son senequistas" ("Seneca Was Not a Spaniard, nor Are Spaniards Followers of Seneca"), Castro refutes the notion of the affinity between the Stoic philosophy of Seneca and the allegedly sober and self-denying nature of the Spanish people (pp. 642–45). This parallel is so pervasive among Spanish historians, critics, and literary figures (Francisco de Quevedo, Marcelino Menéndez y Pelayo, Miguel de Unamuno, and especially Angel Ganivet) that it has become an accepted facet of the Spanish national character. Castro argues, however, that Seneca's birth in what later became a Spanish city is no basis for drawing a parallel between Roman Stoicism and Spanish resignation. He further points out that the Spaniards who evoke the spirit of Seneca do not even penetrate the surface of his philosophy, for if they did, they would find little similarity. If Spaniards had been followers of Seneca, he declares, everything about them (their behavior, their customs) would have been different from what it is: their world view would have focused on this life and not on otherworldly matters (p. 642). Castro provides the material for Goytisolo, in whose hands all those who evoke the stoicism of the Spanish national character, including Seneca himself, become objects of a bitter parody.[5]

Yet Goytisolo's affinity with Castro is more than an intellectual alignment that continues the historian's line of argument. In *Don Julián* and later in *Juan sin tierra,* Goytisolo oversteps the bounds of Castro's view of Spanish reality by adding new factors to that reality. Of these new elements perhaps the most important is sexuality, the vindication of the human body through language. In a collection of his most recent essays titled *Disidencias,* Goytisolo shows his interest in the relationship between sexuality and language. One of these essays offers an intricate analysis of one of Spain's most controversial texts—*La Celestina.*[6] The article is a laudatory appraisal of a study by Stephen Gilman that follows Castro's line of argument on *La Celestina.*[7] Goytisolo allies himself with Castro and Gilman who both see the work as a pessimistic and tragic statement on the human condition, a depiction of a world in which there is no order, no meaning, and no moral justice.

There is a subtle incongruity, however, between the Castro–Gilman analysis and that of Goytisolo. Throughout his discussion, Goytisolo stresses the violence of *La Celestina,* an element that also interests Gilman intensely. In the final section of the article, the theme of violence turns to the theme of sexuality. Goytisolo brings to light the full consequences of what he believes to be Gilman's and Castro's analyses: since human beings are ultimately alone in Rojas's literary world and have no ideal or God on which to base a higher order, the only factors on which people may rely are their instinctual and egotistical urges. In Goytisolo's view, the violence of the hidden self, sexual desires, and base instincts are positive affirmations of life. Goytisolo sees *La Celestina* as an expression of sexual freedom, as a cry for the liberation of the human body reminiscent of the marquis de Sade.

> Rojas, como tres siglos más tarde Sade, reivindica la primacia de la impulsación erótica y su también ciega inexorable furia . . . El caos, la incomunicación, la soledad desembocan asimismo en *La Celestina*, en la afirmación soberana de un egoísmo que no tiene en cuenta los "impulsos debilitantes" de la piedad, gratitud o afecto, ni se sacrifica a lo que Sade denomina "simulacros": Dios, ideal, el prójimo. (pp. 28–29)

> (Rojas, like Sade three centuries ago, reclaims the primacy and blind, inexorable fury of the erotic impulse . . . In *La Celestina*, chaos, noncommunication, solitude all lead to the sovereign affirmation of a self that does not consider the "debilitating impulses" of pity, gratitude, or affection, nor does it yield to what Sade calls "their simulacra": God, the ideal, one's fellow man.)

Goytisolo's writing of *Don Julián* is, in many ways, his reading and extension of Castro. The second volume of the trilogy exposes the implication of Castro's analysis and thereby renders ambiguous the discussion of historical reality. Linda Levine and others have called Goytisolo a "mythoclast," an exponent of Castro's destruction of the Spanish self-concept. This view, while not incorrect, is incomplete.[8] Unlike Castro, Goytisolo actively and consciously participates in the creation of a new mythology that will be an alternative to the beliefs, values, customs, and habits that are repugnant to him. In such an undertaking there is no pretense of offering the real picture of Spanish culture and history, for the old, abhorrent myths are just as real (or unreal) as the new ones. Don Julián, the count of Ceuta, is recast: he is transported from 711 into a contemporary setting, and his story is retold in a way that creates a totally new Don Julián who stands in direct contrast to the old one. In Goytisolo's novel the old and new Don Juliáns struggle against each other, as the modern-day count tries desperately to distort and subvert the fiber of the original myth. Yet the old myth remains intact as the new one emerges. The outcome of this never-ending battle is ambiguous. Reality becomes lost in the linguistic re-creation and interplay between an old mythology and a new one.

Intertextuality is the source of both the concept and the technique that allow for the creative destruction of the anti-Moorish Spanish essence. Intertextuality encompasses Goytisolo's new conception of Spain and of writing. Writing has become an act of treason, but it remains a conscious process of linguistic manipulation in which other texts are altered in order to create a certain effect. This concept of writing also questions the feasibility of the type of social criticism found in *El pasado efímero,* for it undermines the notion of reality implied in the early works. Goytisolo's act of aggression against his country is not directed toward the reality of that society, toward the social or economic conditions of contemporary Spain. Instead, he submerges his critique of peninsular life into a textual field; all reality in *Don Julián* is literary. Because of the intertextual nature of the work, reading *Don Julián* as a reenactment of a historical event becomes insufficient; the book should be viewed instead as the rewriting of the historical and literary texts that describe that event.

Immediately after the title page of *Don Julián*, there are three quotations that serve as the dominant intertexts for the rest of the work. The first is a modern, historical account of the Arab conquests in the seventh and eighth centuries from *Historia de España* by Luis de Valdeavellano.[9] The historian expresses uncertainty about the real name and origin of Conde don Julián.

En lucha con los Bizantinos y los Bereberes, los caudillos militares árabes van extendiendo sus dominios africanos y ya en el año 682 Uqba había llegado al Atlántico, pero no pudo ocupar Tánger, obligado a desviarse hacia el Atlas por un misterioso personaje al que los historiadores musulmanes llaman casi siempre Ulyan y que probablemente se llamara Julián o quizás Urbano, Ulbán o Bulian. De él se iba a apoderar pronto la leyenda con el nombre de "Conde don Julián." (p. xv)

(In their struggle against the Byzantines and the Berbers, the Arab chieftains had greatly extended their African dominions, and as early as the year 682 Uqba had reached the shores of the Atlantic, but he was unable to occupy Tangier, for he was forced to turn back toward the Atlas Mountains by a mysterious person whom Moslem historians always refer to as Ulyan, though his real name was probably Julian, or perhaps Urban, Ulbán, or Bulian. Soon thereafter, he became a legendary figure, known as "Count Julian.")

Goytisolo takes advantage of this vacillation by creating a protagonist who constantly changes identities (from Julián to the seductive serpent, from the *yo* to the *tú*, and from Ulyán to Ulbán). This subject appears in a situation that resembles that of the Conde don Julián described by Valdeavellano.

The second quotation, an excerpt from Alfonso the Wise's *Crónica general*,[10] also serves as one of the crucial texts to which Goytisolo's re-creation of Don Julián stands in opposition.

> Maldita sea la saña del traidor Julián ca mucho fué perseverada; maldita sea la su ira, ca mucho fué dura et mala, ca sandio fué él con su ravia et corajoso con su incha, antuviado con su locura, olbidado de lealdad, desacordado de la ley, despreciador de Dios, cruel en sí mismo, matador de su señor, enemigo de su casa, destroidor de su tierra, culpado et alevoso et traidor contra todos los suyos; amargo es el su nombre en la boca de quil nombra . . . e el su nombre siempre será maldito de quantos dél fablaren. (p. xvii)

> (Accursed be the fury of the traitor Julian, of which we were long the victims; accursed be his wrath, for it was cruel and evil; his rage was boundless and his hatred intractable, his madness precocious; he was incapable of loyalty, respected no law of the land, and scorned God; a pitiless man, the murderer of his suzerain, the enemy of his own house, the destroyer of his own land, perfidious and treacherous and guilty of many grave misdeeds against his own people; there is a bitter ring to his name in the mouths of those who utter it . . . and his name will be forever accursed by all who mention it.)

All that is negative, perverse, blasphemous, cruel, and treasonous in Alfonso's *Crónica* is seen in a new light. In Goytisolo's hands, Don Julián's perversity, cruelty, and disloyalty become positive qualities.

The third quotation, which is from the marquis de Sade, is closest to Goytisolo's text in that it also stands in opposition to the historical texts (p. xvii): "Je voudrais trouver un crime dont l'effet perpétuel agît . . . au point qui'il entraînât une corruption générale ou un dérangement si formel qu'au delà même de ma vie l'effet s'en prolongeât encore" ("I should like to discover a crime the effect of which would be actively felt forever, . . . which would then spread so widely as to bring on such general corruption or such absolute disruption that the effect of it would be prolonged beyond my own lifetime"). Sade's search for the self-perpetuating crime is, in effect, the search undertaken by Julián in Goytisolo's text. These three passages introduce *Don Julián* and anticipate the works that appear within it.

The version of the story of Count Julián in the *Historia de España,* Alfonso the Wise's moral declamation, and the indirect reference to the new Don Julián in Sade are disguised throughout Goytisolo's novel in the form of specific literary, historical, and journalistic texts, each of which exposes its unique rendition of the story. The references to the writings of the Generation of '98, the historical analyses of Ramón Menéndez Pidal and Claudio Sánchez Albornoz (archrival of Castro), and the Spanish press all in some way relate to the account of Count Julián's treason at the turn of the eighth century. Throughout Goytisolo's discourse on the legend of Count Julián, the reader apprehends the author's subversion of a variety of Spanish texts.

The treatment of the texts of Goytisolo's literary tradition takes two basic forms: commentary and parody. The first, by no means a reasoned academic discussion of Spanish literature, is, on the contrary, a tirade against the "great" achievements of Spanish authors. This commentary is hidden behind fictional situations and events that are subordinate to the cited texts and literary figures. A textual allusion is not a device in the service of a guiding idea or theme; it *is* the theme, the actual subject of discourse. Commentary may follow the citation of a previous text, or it may take the form of a reminiscence of a theme, character, or a motif from an outside text.

In parody, Goytisolo reproduces the style and intent of previous Spanish texts for his own ulterior motives; in essence, through parody, he corrupts the previous author's original direction. Commentary separates the outside text and the main text, but in parody, there is an imitation of the outside text by the main text that results in a merger between them. The voices of both texts resound as we witness a struggle in which neither wins. The ambiguous nature of parody is evidenced in the fusion of the opposing forces: imitation and struggle.

Commentary

One of the situations in *Don Julián* in which there is discourse on literature takes place, appropriately, in a library. As the protagonist wanders around the stacks gazing at the books, Goytisolo takes the opportunity to discuss the masters of Spanish literature.

> los autores de genio y figura : los viscerales, los castizos, los broncos : fósiles, crustáceos, dermatoesqueléticos : fieles a las constantes inde-rogables de vuestro espíritu, a las entretelas jugosas de vuestra alma : Parnasos excelsos, florestas sublimes : soneto, criatura virginal y perfecta, cítara y arpa, dulce violín de musical madera conmovida! : escalando a los niveles superiores gracias a la barra de metal que, paralela al suelo, corre a lo largo de las estanterías y en la que se engancha la escalera de mano : indagando en la necrópolis de los bardos y escogiendo algún recio drama de honor : de Calderón, Tirso o del con razón Vega por lo siempre llano : volviendo de nuevo a tierra y regresando a tu pupitre con el sabroso botín. (p. 36)[11]

> (the authors with genius and the trappings of genius: visceral, noble, tough writers: fossils, crustaceans, all skin and bones: faithful to the inviolable constants of your spirit, the rich texture of your innermost soul: lofty Parnassuses, dense, magnificent anthologies: the sonnet, a virginal, perfect creature, zither and harp, the sweet-sounding violin carved out of mellow, melodious wood: climbing up to the top shelves with the aid of the little ladder running along a metal groove parallel to the floor: exploring the necropolis of bards and choosing a stark drama of honor, by Calderón or Tirso or Lope, the latter so rightly named since his verses are inevitably terribly flat: coming down to earth again and going back to your reading desk with your rich booty.) (pp. 25–26)

In this passage Goytisolo alludes primarily to the Golden Age of Spanish literature and to the Neoplatonic theories of poetry and art. The passage is dominated by the tension between the high esteem in which these "authors with genius" are held and the frequent suggestions of death, decrepitude, and decay. Goytisolo counterposes the first few phrases in which the senescence of the writers is described in biological terms ("viscerales," "crust-áceos," "dermatoesqueléticos") with the subsequent lines, which contain words that evoke the elevated and the sublime ("perfecta," "florestas sublimes," "madera conmovida"). The reference to the Neoplatonic poetic theories of divine imitation (the attempt to ascend to the heavens) appears not only in the direct allusion to the "Parnasos excelsos" but also in the use of musical instruments to describe the sonnet, a common device in Renaissance poetry.[12] In the next lines we return to the scientific and the concrete. The protagonist scales the high levels of the bookshelves with the aid of a ladder resting on a metal bar. He continues his investigation in "la necrópolis de los bardos," chooses a "recio drama de honor," and descends the ladder back to earth. These last lines are reminiscent of the biblical account of Christ's resurrection: the ascension into the heavens of the shelves, the discovery of a work of "great" literature, and the descent back to earth, all occurring on a dusty ladder in the stacks of a library. The comment on Lope undermines the dramatist's stature in Spanish literature with a witty Cervantine pun much in the style of Lope himself ("del con razón Vega por lo siempre llano"). In these lines Goytisolo alludes not only to Lope but also to the triumvirate of the Golden Age "comedia" (Calderón, Tirso, and Lope) as their works are synthesized into one text. This subversive style is consistent with Goytisolo's attempt to debunk the notions of the greatness of these classical texts. The lofty tone and high aesthetic aspirations blend with the low, the biological, and the concrete. The result is a new text that subverts the intentions of the old ones. At the same time, Goytisolo seeks a greater accomplishment than the mere destruction of texts. He wishes to demolish the texts' significance by destroying the way of perceiving the world that underlies them: the concept of honor, the deeply embedded link between religion and writing.

Goytisolo's commentaries frequently transcend the specific work and become an analysis of all Spanish cultural achievements. In these cases the individuals responsible for these achievements, especially the men of letters, come under serious attack. Their writings appear within Goytisolo's text as words and phrases that recall these authors' literary, philosophical, and ethical concerns. In one section (pp. 138–40), the intertextual nature of Goytisolo's commentaries on Spanish intellectuals is evidenced in its totality. In that section, the "illustrious men" are not attacked merely as individuals but as classical writers, the archetypes of Spanish culture. Goytisolo makes specific reference (p. 139) to the works of José Ortega y Gasset ("teórico de la razón vital"), to Ganivet's *Idearium español*, and to Juan Ramón Jiménez's *Platero y yo* ("paladines del Cid, de Séneca, de Platero"), as well as to the Generation of '98, "grupo sin par de estilistas . . . autores de deleitables ensayos" ("incomparable group of stylists . . . authors of delightful essays"). At the same time, the texts of these writers merge into a single collective unit. Goytisolo undermines the reverence in which these writers are held by exaggerating their cultural worth as in (p. 138) "maestros universalmente queridos, admirados, y respetados" ("masters universally cherished and admired and respected," p. 115). He also achieves this by the insertion of the mundane into his ironic praise (pp. 139–40): "del españolísimo vínculo existente entre el estoicismo y la tauromaquia . . . opuestos al time is money . . . enemigos viscerales del Baedeker y el sleeping car, de las almohadas y del baño : del ferrocarril, del watercloset, del teléfono" ("of the intimate, typically Spanish linking between stoicism and tauromachy [the theory of bullfighting] . . . very Hispanically opposed to time-is-money . . . visceral enemies of Baedeker and the sleeping car, pillows, and bathrooms: of railroads, the flush toilet, and the telephone," pp. 116–17). The blend of elevated praise with the mundane, the high with the low, is a constant in Goytisolo's work.

One of the most common ways in which Goytisolo integrates other texts with his own is by turning the famous men of Spanish letters into characters and placing them in situations that undermine their greatness. The subversion is accomplished with fictional characters that are creations of literature (Sancho Panza, Platero, Little Red Riding Hood, figures from the Bible and Greek mythology as well as re-creations of the "great" authors themselves). In one instance (p. 116), a character who is reminiscent of Unamuno is found behind a table covered with books, papers, "y un austero crucifijo Kierkegaardiano" ("and an austere Kierkegaardian crucifix"). As Goytisolo focuses closer, the character unfolds a cape and begins waving it about like a bullfighter:

> severo y enjuto mientras despliega gravemente la muleta y realiza una serie inigualable de manoletinas y pases de pecho que provocan el sobrecogedor deliquio, el arrobo seráfico de la hispana multitud : acogiendo las delirantes aclamaciones con un rictus estereotipado y llevándose la mano, esa personalísima mano suya que parece pintada por El Greco, al sitio del corazón ah, me duele España! (pp. 116–17)

> (stern-faced, lean, and spare, slowly spreading his cape and executing an unsurpassable series of "manoletinas" and "pases de pecho" which provoke the awed surprise, the seraphic ecstasy of the multitudes from one end of the Peninsula to the other: acknowledging the delirious applause with a stereotyped rictus, raising his hand, that most unusual hand, unlike any other, which might have been painted by El Greco, to the general region of his heart
> oh, my Spain hurts me) (p. 97)

In addition to Unamuno's philosophy (which in turn refers to the work of Kierkegaard), Goytisolo alludes to a painting by El Greco *(El caballero de la mano en el pecho)* and indirectly to Ortega y Gasset's *La caza y los toros (Hunting and Bullfighting)*.[13] The character described in this passage assumes the identities of all these figures: Unamuno, Kierkegaard, El Greco's noble *caballero,* and Seneca, whom Goytisolo frequently portrays as a bull-fighter—for example (p. 115), "el pequeño Séneca aprende rápidamente los pases de la filosofía de salón y . . . se traslada a la universidad taurina de Salamanca" ("little Seneca rapidly learns the passes required for philosophical duels in salons and . . . he transfers to the taurine University of Salamanca," p. 96). As Goytisolo blends all these figures into a single textual expression of the Spanish essence, he ridicules the concept of national cultural unity. Through the integration of these varied entities (a popular bullfighter and the severe Seneca), Goytisolo demolishes the pedestal on which these figures and texts have been placed.

The demythification of Spanish literary figures continues through the presence of Seneca in a variety of situations. In his re-creation of Seneca as a character, Goytisolo reinforces the ancient philosopher's significance to Spanish history as analyzed by Ganivet in the *Idearium español*. According to Ganivet, Seneca symbolizes the righteousness of the Spanish national character. He declares at one point that Seneca was not a Spaniard by birth and most certainly was not an Andalusian (since modern Andalusians have no connection with those who lived in southern Spain during Seneca's time), but that he was nonetheless a Spaniard "in essence," in his world view. He warned people never to yield to something alien to their spirit. For Ganivet, Seneca was not rigid but compassionate. He promulgated the laws of virtue to which all people should adhere, but he was tolerant of those who were unable to live up to them.[14]

The *Idearium español,* one of Spain's most sacred books, is for Goytisolo and for virtually all historians of Spanish literature a precursor to the essays of the Generation of '98 that expressed the search for a definition of the Spanish national spirit. In *Don Julián* Seneca presides over a variety of cultural activities that at first glance seem to have nothing to do with Stoic philosophy: bullfighting (p. 162)—"senequismo de Manolete" ("the Senecism of Manolete," p. 137); censorship (p. 205)—"vuestra castiza y españolísima teoría de la información" ("your mythical and quintessentially Spanish theory of information," p. 173); and the pathological negation of the human body (a constant motif in *Don Julián*). At one point,

> Séneca esboza un ademán de disculpa y, como tú callas, prosigue su discurso con énfasis yo mismo, en trance semejante, he redactado alguna de mis mejores epístolas a Lucilio : en particular aquella tan famosa sobre los deseos inmoderados, la recuerda usted?
> no, no la recuerdas
> es lástima, dice él : en ella pulverizo las tesis de Freud, Marx y Federico Nietzsche : por cierto, sabía usted que este último era sifilítico? (p. 154)

> (Seneca gives a vague apologetic wave of his hand, and since you say nothing in reply, he continues his discourse in an emphatic tone of voice
> it was at a similar critical moment that I myself composed some of my best epistles to Lucilius: the famous one on intemperate desires, for one particular instance: do you remember it?
> no, you do not remember it

that's a shame, he remarks: in it I utterly demolish the hypotheses of Freud, Marx, and Friedrich Nietzsche: I suppose you know that the latter was a syphilitic?) (p. 129)

Given the context in which these elevated words are uttered—the philosopher admits that his epistle was written while he was urinating or defecating—Goytisolo has subverted the accepted view of Seneca's greatness and his affinity with sacred Spain. The philosopher's diction becomes more and more vulgar as the conversation continues. He tells the protagonist that Nietzsche's syphilis inspired him to write an ode for which he was awarded "medio millón de pesetejas!" by the Al Capone Foundation (p. 154). Finally, Seneca's speech degenerates into street dialect as he invites the protagonist to indulge in the delights of a whore who lives nearby (p. 155): "dieciocho añines, y, en la cama, una fiera: francesa ella, y eso sí : limpia y educá: si quiés medirle el aceite, te la presento : casualmente vive cerca de aquí : veinticinco dirhames por un rato, cincuenta toa la noche : vienes, macho?" ("barely eighteen, and a real tigress in bed: an honest-to-goodness French girl: very clean, with nice manners: if you'd care to measure how much oil she's got in her lamp, I'd be glad to introduce her to you: it wouldn't be any trouble at all: she lives right here in the neighborhood: twenty-five dirherms a lay, fifty for the whole night: what do you say, fellah?," p. 130). Seneca's frequent appearances, along with the various identities that he assumes (Unamuno, Seneca Junior, Seneca Senior, a bullfighter, Franco, the Figurón, Don Alvaro, an electoral candidate), allow him to become not only a symbol of sacred Spain but also a myth. He is part of a mythology that defines "the Spain of yesterday, today, and tomorrow."[15] This mythology manifests itself through texts of all sorts as they are picked apart and as their signification is corrupted.

In *Don Julián* the attempted demolition of a greater part of the Spanish literary tradition takes on new force because certain texts from this tradition are aids in the author's creative-destructive enterprise. The discourse on these dissenting or "positive" texts[16] pays homage to what Goytisolo views as their destructive and heterodox spirit. In this case, Goytisolo again reads (or misreads) these texts as representations of his own interests and intentions. His writing becomes a self-reading, an activity in which he identifies his intentions with those of other writers. The presence of Luis de Góngora and Larra in *Don Julián* evidences the crucial importance of this type of laudatory discourse. The linguistic manipulation in the baroque poetry of Góngora serves as an inspiration to Goytisolo. He draws Góngora into his text as the archetypal "Poeta" (p. 124): "altivo, gerifalte, Poeta, ayúdame : a luz más cierta súbeme" ("soaring falcon, noble Poet, come to my aid: bear me aloft to the realm of more luminous truths," p. 104). The use of the second-person command combined with rhyme and the typically baroque Gongorine conceit (the noun *gerifalte* used to modify the noun *Poeta*) are the main elements of a commentary that is unique in that it exists within the text as the exception to Goytisolo's view of Spanish literature. There is an allusion to Góngora at one point where the protagonist is found gazing toward the coast of Spain from a mirador on a beach in Tangier (p. 68): "árbitro de montañas y ribera, diría el Poeta : saludando, aliviado, la presencia difusa del mar : que separa una orilla de otra y libera tu tierra de adopción de la acuciante, venenosa cicatriz" ("the sovereign arbiter of mountain peaks and the ocean strand, as the Poet would say: greeting, with a feeling of relief, the diffuse presence of the sea separating this shore from the other and guarding your adoptive country against the painful, poisonous scar," pp. 54–55). This intricate geographical description is evocative of the opening of Góngora's *Soledad primera,* in which the shipwrecked pilgrim finds himself on a strange, deserted beach where the objects of nature (rocks, the ocean, the sun) have human qualities. The straits that separate Spain from Africa are in Goytisolo's text a mediation between two opposites, and at the same time, they divide and liberate the "tierra de adopción" (Africa) from what is poisonous, painful, and dazzling (Spain). Goytisolo's comparison of the straits with a wound or scar is a conceit found at other points in *Don Julián;* in this case (p. 68), it materializes the alliance between the two texts. Later the author explicitly evokes Góngora's language, which is necessary for Julián's planned betrayal of everything Spanish (p. 70): "idioma mirífico del Poeta, vehículo necesario de la traición, hermosa lengua tuya : instrumento indispensable del renegado y del apóstata, esplendoroso y devastador a la vez : arma aguda (insinuante) que conjura (exorcisa) la africana hueste y magnifica (potencia) su denso apetito de destrucción" ("the marvelous language of the Poet, the linguistic vehicle most appropriate for treason, your beautiful native tongue: the indispensable weapon of the renegade and the apostate, at once magnificent and devastating: a sharp-pointed (insidious) weapon that drives off (exorcises) the African army and increases (whets) its irresistible appetite for destruction," p. 56). This combination of commentary on and imitation of Góngora produces an instrument of perverse destruction. The tribute to the "Poeta," the incorporation of his verbal manipulation into the text, and the added dimensions of betrayal, exorcism, and devastation form an unholy alliance of destruction. The languages of Góngora and Goytisolo have, in effect, become one; the unity of the two styles is the "indispensable weapon" needed to commit this treason.

In much the same way, Larra represents for Goytisolo another literary exception, another writer who is read as an affirmation of Goytisolo's personal direction. Goytisolo continues the spirit of Larra through commentaries on the romantic writer's political and social essays. Although social criticism in the tradition of the nineteenth-century realists is virtually nonexistent, there is a vehement type of social criticism in *Don Julián*. But, since Goytisolo's social reality is the reality of the written word, he must rely on other texts, such as Larra's, whose social direction blends with his own. Toward the beginning of *Don Julián*, Goytisolo alludes to one of Larra's articles, "El hombre-globo" ("The Balloon Man," also a pun on "global," "universal"). The ironic structure of this essay, including the use of the vocabulary of the physical sciences to assess a social and political situation, appears within Goytisolo's introductory description of his protagonist and of the atmosphere in which he finds himself. Goytisolo uses Larra's comparison of human elements with those of the physical sciences (solid, liquid, and gas) and elaborates on them (p. 21): "abajo el sólido de los sólidos : costra del mundo, base del edificio social . . . en medio, el hombre líquido : corriendo y serpenteando encima del anterior . . . en la cúspide, la ártica región del pensamiento : el hombre-gas, el hombre-globo" ("at the very bottom, the most solid of solids: the earth's crust, the base of the social edifice . . . in the middle, man-the-liquid, meandering across the stratum beneath . . . at the very top, the Arctic realm of thought: man-the-gas, man-the-moon," p. 12). In Larra's essay these physical qualities are also the characteristics of certain types of human beings. Larra leads his reader to believe that the predominance of certain of these characteristics is the cause of an unfavorable social and political situation.[17] Goytisolo, however, allows these states of physical matter to stand alone. There are fewer references to human beings; therefore greater importance is attached to the concrete scientific object that only indirectly points to something human. The remainder of the section deals with people, but again Goytisolo's depiction is far more concrete than Larra's. He limits himself to specific examples of the solid stratum of society. The blind man, the little old woman, the beggars, the victims of the petty tyrants, the people who do not fight back are all victims of a sickness whose cause goes far beyond the social order. The roots of the infirmity are found in the historical rejection and negation of Arab culture, in the supremacy of Spain over Africa.

The infection (p. 23)—"contaminado del castizo y militar ambiente del paternalismo familiar y bronco de los de tu fauna" ("contaminated by the aristocratic, military atmosphere, the brusque, condescending paternalism that fauna of your species live amid," p. 13)—is later offset by another kind of poison—that of Julián in his call to arms as he invokes the reconquest of Spain by the Arabs. In this undertaking Julián is a perverse and malicious disciple of Larra. The character's search for the origins of the sickness ends in a rediscovery of language, for in Larra's essays, Goytisolo finds an embodiment of his own writing. Larra's criticism is, in Goytisolo's eyes, linguistic as well as social—an attempt to degrade the social order through the contamination of its language. Thus Goytisolo's commentary on Larra reveals another example of self-reading, a desire to identify Larra's writing with his own act of linguistic contamination.

Parody

According to José Ortega, parody plays an important role in *Don Julián*. Yet Ortega's cursory analysis of intertextuality in Goytisolo sheds no light on the problem of parody as a unique form of writing or on Goytisolo's particular use of it.[18] If one wishes to apprehend Goytisolo's parodies, one must first come to terms with the theory of parody implicit in his work. Goytisolo's stated interest in Russian formalist literary criticism[19] illuminates this crucial aspect of his writing. Yuri Tynyanov, Roman Jakobson, and Boris Eichenbaum all touched on a theory of parody, but their discussion was not carried to its full consequences until Mikhail Bakhtin wrote his insightful book, *Problems in Dostoevsky's Poetics*.[20] Parody is subsumed into Bakhtin's notion of "dialogical writing." This concept embodies a collision or conflict between words, a relationship that also applies to opposing texts and, at times, to texts within texts. "Thus dialogical relationships can penetrate an utterance, or even an individual word, so long as two voices collide within it" (p. 152). This collision of directions (a collision between texts) is the essence of parody. Bakhtin states that in parody the author

> introduces a semantic direction into that word, [another person's word] which is diametrically opposed to its original direction. The second voice, which has made its home in the other person's word, collides in a hostile fashion with the original owner and forces him to serve purposes diametrically opposed to his own. The word becomes the arena of conflict between two voices. Therefore, the merging of voices, as can occur in stylization or in the narrator's story . . . is impossible in the parody: the voices here are not only detached and distanced, they are hostilely counterposed. (p. 160)

The emphasis on semantic hostility within one word is highly pertinent to Goytisolo's use of parody. Rather than an open commentary on a previous text in which the semantic struggle is evident, the war between words in parody is covert. The battle remains within one word or phrase that reminds us of a previous text and subverts its original direction. According to this definition, parody is perhaps the most appropriate tool for Goytisolo's undertaking. His parodies serve as the models for the invasion of the mother country. *Don Julián* is the arena of conflict between the old and the new, between traditional and contemporary Spain, between the Spanish literary legacy and the attempt to destroy that legacy. In many ways, the work in its totality is a parody of the whole of Spanish literary production.

Bakhtin's discussion of the concrete forms of parody is perfectly applicable to *Don Julián,* whether the book is seen as a container of specific parodies or as one all-encompassing parody.

> The parodistic word can be extremely diverse. Another person's style can be parodied as a style; another person's social-typical or individual-charonterological manner of seeing, thinking and speaking can be parodied. . . . one can parody only superficial verbal forms, or one can parody the deepest principles of the other person's word. Furthermore, the parodistic word itself can be employed by the author in various ways: parody can be an end in itself (the literary parody as a genre, for example), but it can also serve other, positive purposes. (pp. 160–61)

The essayists of the Generation of '98 are one of the most frequent objects of parody in *Don Julián.* Apart from the instances in which Goytisolo transforms novelistic narration into discourse on these writers, there are many points where he mimicks their style and concerns and, thereby, corrupts their original intentions. The descriptions of the eternally austere plains of Castile and the evocations of the nature of the Spanish people are degraded and rendered laughable. The library is again the setting for one of these parodies. Goytisolo allows his protagonist to leaf through the volumes of essays on the geography and national character of Spain written by the writers of '98:

> estrellas fijas del impoluto firmamento hispano : del espíritu unido por las raíces a lo eterno de la casta : prosapia de hoy, de ayer y de

mañana, asegurada siglo a siglo por solar y ejecutoria de limpios y honrados abuelos : desde Indíbil, Séneca y Lucano hasta la pléyade luminosa de varones descubridores de la ancestral esencia histórica, del escueto, monoteístico paisaje : Castilla! : llanuras pardas, páramos huesosos, descarnadas peñas erizadas de riscos : seca, dura, sarmentosa : extensas y peladas soledades : patria rezumando pus y grandeza por entre agrietadas costras de cicatrices : obra colectiva de esa preclara generación. (p. 34)

(the fixed stars of the pure Hispanic firmament: of the Spanish spirit rooted in the basic, enduring truths of an entire people: the lineage of yesterday, today, and tomorrow, a patrimony and titles of nobility handed down for century after century by the most honorable and upright forebears: from Indíbel, Seneca, and Lucan to the brightly gleaming constellation of men who discovered the very essence of your historical heritage, the barren, monotheistic landscape: Castile!: gray plains, bony wastelands, bare crags bristling with rocks: dry, hard, gnarled: vast, lonely, naked expanses: a homeland oozing pus and grandeur through the cracked crusts of its wounds: the collective work of an illustrious generation.) (p. 24)

Goytisolo wishes to draw attention to Unamuno's *En torno al casticismo (Castilianism)*, [21] a work that was, by Unamuno's own admission, inspired by Ganivet's *Idearium*.[22] The passage alludes to *Casticismo* through the evocation of certain concepts expressed in Unamuno's work and by the use of words and phrases taken directly from it (pp. 109–11): "Son estribaciones de huesosas y descarnadas peñas erizadas de riscos" ("They are spurs of bony bare crags bristling with rocks"); "paisaje monoteístico" ("monotheistic landscape"); "imponente monotonía" ("imposing monotony"); "una casta de complexión seca, dura y sarmentosa" ("a caste of a dry, hard, and gnarled complexion"). In Goytisolo's text "lo eterno de la casta" and "prosapia de hoy de ayer y de mañana" (p. 34) refer to Unamuno's concept of the Spanish *intra-historia,* the spiritual characteristics, the *casta,* that bind together Castilians and all Spaniards. Thus the passage is both a synthesis of the original text and an undoing of it. The exclamatory, "Castilla!," the title of Unamuno's second chapter, breaks the previous text down into one expression. In like manner, Unamuno's subtle comparison between the plains of Castile and the heavens—"our Castilian World of lofty clouds, a planetary system of ideas" (p. 814)—is reinforced in Goytisolo. But in the latter, the comparison is stated with such clarity that it begins to subvert Unamuno's poetic intentions. A vocabulary of astronomy is used by Goytisolo to describe the Castilian essence: "estrellas fijas" ("fixed stars"); "firmamento hispano" ("Hispanic firmament"); and the play on words, "pléyade luminosa" ("luminous constellation"), which in Spanish signifies both a constellation and a group of renowned poets. Further, there is an allusion to Unamuno's Christian existentialism (a religious vision that is full of contradictions, tensions, and doubts) in the "monoteístico paisaje," which not only signifies a fixed religious ideology but also suggests monotony and boredom. The Spanish philosopher's "man of flesh and bone," one of the principal motifs of his *Del sentimiento trágico de la vida (Tragic Sense of Life),* is turned into "páramos huesosos" ("bony wastelands") and "descarnadas peñas" ("bare crags"). Loneliness, another of Unamuno's motifs evoking a sense of tragedy, becomes objectified into barrenness and sterility. Goytisolo's last image blends geography and humanity as Unamuno does, yet in Goytisolo, the effect is remarkably different. For Unamuno, the harsh landscape defines the lofty, serene, and honorable goals of the Spanish race; for Goytisolo, the rocky crusts are wounds creating their own pus. The tension within the passage between "pus" (the biological) and "grandeur" (the spiritual) expresses the tension between the two texts.

A further aspect of Goytisolo's manipulation of Unamuno's *En torno al casticismo* is the inversion of the object of literary creation into the literary creation of the object. Unamuno's language evokes geography as a creator of deeply rooted national characteristics by describing the way in which geography affects the Spanish soul. In Goytisolo, however, geography is created in the act of writing. The clean and honorable ancestors discover the landscape and thus create their own historical essence. The fact that the passage alludes to an established literary tradition renders the written word the only objective reality: the description of the landscape creates the landscape itself. All the objects of parody (the rocks, the crusts, the plains) are the collective creation of the writers of this "preclara [illustrious] generación."

In part 3 of *Don Julián*, the parody of the literary production of the Generation of '98 continues but in a harsher way. Julián has already begun the invasion; the gateway to the peninsula has been opened as the Arabs "gallop" (p. 142) over the Castilian plain, destroying all in their path. The collision between texts is violent: the subversion, indirect and subtle in part 1, is painfully evident in part 3. The sterility, starkness, and aridity of the plains are to be wiped out as Julián attempts to alter the climate that causes the lack of vegetation (p. 146): "amontarás masas de nubes que convulsionarán bruscamente el clima" ("you will heap up masses of clouds that will cause a sudden, violent change of climate," p. 123). The result:

> adiós paisajes áridos, páramos infecundos, planicies sedientas! : los efluvios éticos han cesado : vuestra desnudez dejará de alimentar la obscena metafísica : cúmulos, nimbos, cirros, estratos velarán para siempre el cielo : lanaturaleza devendrá lluviosa : barbechos y rastrojos verdearán : cereales, hortalizas, legumbres tapizarán el fértil llano : una laberíntica red de canales impulsará la burlesca transformación : los polders reemplazarán el yermo : sobre un fondo aguanoso y húmedo, las vacas pacerán entre los tulipanes (pp. 146–47)

> (farewell, arid plateaus, barren wastelands, parched plains: the ethical emanations have dried up: your nakedness will cease to nourish the obscene metaphysics: cumulus, nimbus, cirrus, stratus clouds will forever veil the sky: the vegetation will hereafter be that of a rainy region: fallow land and stubble fields will once again be green: strands of grain, vegetable gardens, and orchards will carpet the fertile plain: a network of canals will facilitate this ludicrous transformation: where once there was a wasteland, there will henceforth be polders: within this sodden, soggy setting, cows will graze amid tulips) (p. 123)

In this passage Goytisolo evokes the previous text through contrast, as Julián bids farewell to the language of the essays in an attempt to silence their "ethical discharge." What is "limpio y honrado" in Unamuno now becomes "obscena metafísica"; dryness becomes wetness ("lluviosa," "laberíntica red de canales," "aguanoso y húmedo"); sterility has been transformed into a "fértil llano" in which "cereales, hortalizas, legumbres" have changed the very color of the scenery from white and grey to green. This "burlesca transformación" continues in a similar passage that follows this one. Yet in that passage Goytisolo degrades the Generation of '98 (Unamuno, Azorín [José Martínez Ruiz], even Antonio Machado) with grotesque invectives against a "poeta." In contrast to Goytisolo's "Poeta" (Góngora), this "poeta" assumes the identity of all those Spanish writers who have attempted to create an eternal Spanish essence through the evocation of the Castilian landscape. In addition to the work of Unamuno, the passage indirectly refers to Azorín's essays in *Los pueblos* and *Una hora de España* and to Machado's volume of poetry, *Campos de Castilla*.[23] Of this "poeta," Julián exclaims (p. 147): "que su estómago críe ranas : que su alma germine sapos : que su grotesco cuerpo flote y sea pasto de sanguijuelas" ("may his belly harbor frogs: may his soul engender toads: may his grotesque body drift on the waters and become food for the leeches," p. 123). The parody has reached its climax in the unmitigated contrast between the lyrical descriptions of the Castilian landscapes and the grotesque body images.

The indirect allusions to the works of Hispanists such as Menéndez y Pelayo, Menéndez Pidal, and Sánchez Albornoz, as well as the immediate renditions of political and cultural events in the Spanish press, serve not only to ridicule these scholarly and journalistic works but also to question their existence as separate categories of writing. The pretense of truth, a characteristic of all forms of historical writing, and the way in which the writer removes himself or herself from the events through the use of the third person and the past tense are the objects of ridicule in Goytisolo's parodic rewriting. The parody of historical texts consists primarily of a transformation of history into discourse, that is, from truth to ideology. Goytisolo accepts and comments on the political reality that produced these texts. The situation of the Spanish press (censorship, the forced praise of the Franco regime) creates a unique acceptance of the truth of the written word. The frequent allusions to the *ABC* and to other news periodicals are typical of Goytisolo's debunking of social reality as it is described in the press. In one case he creates a Holy Week procession as it would be reported in a widely read Madrid newspaper (p. 182): "la hispana teoría sale de la iglesia de Santa María la Mayor precedida de la guardia civil a caballo en uniforme de gala : siete mil adoradores de la Adoración Nocturna con sus cruces, ciriales, pendones, banderas" ("the Hispanic procession emerges from the church of Santa María la Mayor, preceded by the Guardia Civil on horseback in dress uniform: seven thousand faithful worshipers of the Nocturnal Adoration with their crosses, their tapers, their pennants, their banners," p. 154). As the procession continues, Goytisolo inserts bits of information about the chains that the penitents drag along the street (p. 183): "diez mil kilos de hierro, fair ladies and good gentlemen! : cadenas adquiridas en el Rastro al precio equivalente de ocho $ cuarenta y cinco centavos o alquiladas a dólar por noche en las ferreterías ante la extraordinaria demanda de última hora, cuando el surtido normal se reveló insuficiente!" ("ten thousand kilos of iron, fair ladies and good gentlemen! chains purchased at the Flea Market for the equivalent of $8.45 (U.S. currency) or rented for a dollar a night at local hardware stores because the last-minute demand for them was enormous and the normal supply was nowhere near enough!," p. 155).[24] The use of the English language, the dollar sign, and the North American *centavos* instead of *pesetas* not only ridicules the account of the event but also reveals its ideological motives (money) and thus negates any pretense of historical objectivity.

The Spanish press is further parodied in Goytisolo's rewriting of editorials, a type of text that is by definition ideological. The lofty tone of this writing, which is typical of Spanish journalism under Franco, tends to overwhelm the ideological content (the opinions) and to emphasize the reality or truth of what is written; in short, through the style of writing, the political and social opinions expressed in the editorials become dogma. But Goytisolo reverses the process. In one case (p. 187), we find an editorial whose flowery tone is representative of the ideology of the *Opus Dei* (a religious organization of technocrats who assumed the

responsibility for the modernization of Spain within the framework of the dictatorship): "decididamente la situación no puede
prolongarse : los técnicos mejorarán las estructuras : nuestra
vocación es europea y la encíclia nos indica el camino :
dialoguemos mezzo voce para instruir al pueblo : los ordenadores
eliminarán con sus cálculos las aparentes contradicciones de
clase" ("this situation definitely cannot continue: technical experts
will improve the structures: our destiny is European and the
encyclical shows us on the way: let us conduct a *mezza voce*
dialogue to educate the people: computer calculations will
eliminate the apparent class contradictions," p. 159). Goytisolo
mocks the words of the *Opus* spokesmen with the insertion of
high-sounding religious words ("nuestra vocación," "encíc-
lica") that are not appropriate for a political editorial in these
secular times. The ironic signification attached to the word
dialoguemos further ridicules the language of the status quo.
Dialogue presupposes the participation of at least two voices, but
only one voice is heard ("dialoguemos . . . para instruir al
pueblo"); the *Opus Dei* talks, the people listen. The concept of
dialogue is counterposed by its opposite—doctrine.[25] Goytisolo's
commentary that precedes the rewriting gives the previous text a
context that delivers the ultimate blow (p. 187): "pensando en
self-made-men, sí, pero con el inconfundible acento de chuleta
de Madrid" ("thinking like self-made men, to be sure, but with
the unmistakable accent of the Madrid street urchin," p. 158).
The tone of the editorial is corrupted by the accent, the
intonation, and the inflections of this Madrilenean *chuleta* (a play
on a word that signifies both "pork chop," referring to the
speaker, and, in the slang of Madrid, a tool for cheating, a crib
sheet). Goytisolo not only annuls the truth of these words with
his *chuleta* (in which the implications of dishonesty are obvious);
he also unites the speaker and the utterance: the speaker, in effect,
has become his words.

Literary criticism, another example of nonfiction writing, is an
object of parody in much the same way as the historical texts are.
Again one may find echoes of the works of erudite Hispanists

(Menéndez Pidal et al.). Goytisolo reads these interpretations of Spanish literature as attempts at absolute definitions of the Spanish historical essence. However, in his parodic manipulation of these academic texts, he destroys all semblances of absolute truth. In one instance, Don Alvaro, a character who is strongly reminiscent of the learned Spanish man of letters, gives a lecture to the Royal Spanish Academy exalting the literature of Spain and the mission of the Spanish people (p. 177): " 'Consideraciones en torno al concepto de honor en el teatro español del siglo XVII' : el estilo es noble, la dicción perfecta" (" 'A Few Remarks on the Concept of Honor in the Seventeenth-Century Spanish Theater': his style is lofty, his diction perfect," p. 149). Don Alvaro speaks, however, with a great deal of uncertainty. His speech is interrupted by a fly that has landed in one of the books and stained one of the pages. He then turns to another book, but the fly has multiplied and metamorphosed into bees, ants, horseflies, and spiders that swarm through the pages devouring the paper, corrupting the style, and infecting the ideas (p. 180). The sexual imagery of the insects copulating—"copulan y se reproducen, se reproducen y copulan"; "entran y salen de los libros" ("they copulate and reproduce, they reproduce and copulate"; "they go in and out of the books")—is evident especially in the light of the most recurrent theme—the rape of Spain by Julián. The effect of the rape is fatal; Don Alvaro is destroyed, robbed of his most essential tool, his language. His breathing becomes labored; he attempts to pronounce a word, but he can only produce a meaningless syllable (p. 181): "cuando el guardián de la biblioteca le cierra los párpados y se descubre, un silencio compacto se establece en la habitación : el hecho no ofrece la menor duda : el caballero ha muerto" ("when the custodian of the library closes Don Alvaro's eyes and respectfully bares his head, a dense silence falls upon the room: there is no possible doubt: the perfect gentleman has died," p. 153). These killer insects, like Goytisolo's perverse manipulation of other texts, are seducers and invaders of the sovereignty of established truth.

The parody of Spanish literary criticism is manifested through the constant presence of these strange insects. Toward the beginning of the work, the protagonist is engaged in an activity much like the act of reading and writing about literature, but his behavior is in no way representative of a scholarly endeavor. While he is in the library he places insects between the pages of the books and slams the covers together, thereby staining the paper (p. 37): "alcanzando el primer volumen de la pila y depositando entre sus páginas una hormiga y seis moscas : en el quintaesenciado diálogo entre Casandra y el duque : esto disponen las leyes de honor, y que no haya publicidad en mi afrenta con que se doble mi infamia : cerrando de golpe, zas!, y aplastándolas" ("reaching for the first volume in the pile and depositing an ant and six flies inside it: in the middle of the crucial scene between Cassandra and the Duke: I could not love thee, dear, so much loved I not honor more: suddenly, closing the volume and crushing these seven insects," p. 26). This unique form of literary criticism is precisely the kind that Goytisolo undertakes in *Don Julián*. Julián's act of vandalism and the author's act of writing show a perverse wish to annihilate the established literary legacy of Spain. Goytisolo has stated that this scene (pp. 36–39) is a parody of an episode from *Don Quijote* in which Cervantes takes the opportunity to offer a critique of books of chivalry and of the literary production of his time through the creation of certain characters ("El escrutinio de los libros").[26] Most of the literature is taken from Don Quijote's library and burned by the barber and the priest in righteous zeal. What is added to Cervantes's situation is the perverse pleasure that Goytisolo's character seems to receive from his deed—the excitement, the fun, the thrill of being malicious (p. 38): "reteniendo apenas la saliva," "ahogando en la garganta el grito de Tarzán," "contento y orgulloso de ti mismo" ("you can hardly keep from drooling," "you stifle a triumphant cry à la Tarzan," "terribly pleased and proud of yourself," p. 27). Cervantes's priest feels that his just deed will cure Don Quijote's madness, but in Goytisolo, the medicinal quality of the purge is enhanced by intense self-gratification.

Goytisolo's inclusion of *Don Quijote* in his long list of parodied texts presents problems for the critic who wishes to come to grips with the intertextual nature of parody, especially in the light of Bakhtin's definition. For the Russian critic, the notion of parody presupposes a clash or conflict between texts, whereas Cervantes seems to stand in alliance with Goytisolo in *Don Julián*. The problem revolves around the parodic structure of *Don Quijote* itself. The conflict between works in "El escrutinio de los libros" is similar to the clash between texts in Goytisolo's scene in the library with one basic difference: Goytisolo enhances and intensifies the struggle that already exists. Thus the treatment of *Don Quijote* in *Don Julián* may be classified as a parody of a parody. Unlike the commentary on Larra and Góngora in which these heterodox Spaniards are solemnly praised, Goytisolo's parody of Cervantes involves the intrusion of his own words within the texts of the writer of the Golden Age. In the citations and imitations of Larra and Góngora, there is no clash of intentions or aesthetic direction, for ultimately all three voices (Larra's, Góngora's, and Goytisolo's) merge into one. The presence of *Don Quijote*, however, is more complex, for there is an attempt to infiltrate and thus to alter the original signification of Cervantes's words.

The similarities between *Don Quijote* and *Don Julián* are evident: they are both books about books, their heroes are both anti-heroes, and both books revolve around a reversal from reality to fantasy and vice versa. The phrase "de cuyo nombre no quiero acordarme" ("whose name I prefer to forget"), taken directly from Cervantes's work, is found at strategic points throughout *Don Julián*. The opening description of Cervantes's protagonist, particularly the narrator's uncertainty about Don Quijote's real name and origin, is brought to mind in the following passage from *Don Julián*:

> español, moro? : joven, viejo? : o alguno de esos enanos velazqueños con quienes tropiezas a menudo en el zoco? : cómo coño saberlo? : en el bullicio musulmán de la calle, pero devuelto a tu infancia y a sus sombríos placeres : veinticinco, veintiséis años? : nueve tenías tú

(si los tenías) y la imagen (inventada o real) pertenece a una ciudad de cuyo nombre no quieres acordarte : la borrarás, pues, y aceptarás de buena gana la diversa, providencial compañía del niño. (p. 60)

(a Spaniard? an Arab? a young man? an old man? or one of those dwarfs straight out of a painting by Velázquez whom you frequently run into in the market place? how in hell will you ever find out?: in the Moorish hustle and bustle of the street, but having at the same time returned to your childhood and its dreary pleasures: twenty-five, twenty-six years ago?: you were nine years old (or almost nine at most) and the image (whether invented or real) is associated with a city, a country whose very name you would prefer to forget: you will therefore erase it from your memory and willingly accept the diverting, providential company of this child.) (p. 47)

The parodic aspects of this passage are apparent not so much in an undoing of the original but in an outdoing of it. Goytisolo puts origin and name into question, as does Cervantes ("Quijada" or "Quesada" or "Quejada"), yet he also attempts to erase what is unfavorable and to keep what he likes, accepting the invention and denying—"borrarás" ("you will erase")—the reality. Thus Goytisolo makes it explicit that the character's past is a purely literary or verbal invention.

At times Goytisolo's use of *Don Quijote* is typically parodic, as there is a diametric opposition in the direction of each text. At one point Goytisolo alludes to the episode in *Don Quijote* in which Sancho becomes the governor of his promised "ínsula." In Cervantes's scene (chapter 47), Sancho's tremendous appetite goes unsatisfied as a result of a doctor's overly cautious orders not to indulge in certain foods. Goytisolo transforms Cervantes's doctor into Julián himself, whom he disguises as a grammarian.

el recio comensal de sanchopanchesca glotonería que aborda su bien surtida mesa con un babador randado y, tras la oración de rigor, se dispone a catar los manjares que le sirven maestresalas y pajes, lo amenazarás con tu varilla de ballena, impuesto de la autoridad y el prestigio de tus severos diplomas lexicográficos
no se ha de comer, señor carpeto [Sancho], sino como es uso y costumbre en las otras ínsulas donde ya he morado : yo, señor, soy gramático, y miro por la pureza del idioma mucho más que por mi vida, estudiando de noche y de día y tanteando la complexión del carpeto para acertar a curarle cuando cayere enfermo : y lo principal que hago es asistir a sus comidas y cenas, y dejarle comer de lo que me

parece castizo y quitarle cuanto etimológicamente es extraño. (p. 197)

(when the diner with a paunch as round as Sancho Panza's and a gluttonous appetite sits down at the groaning board, with a damask napkin tucked under his chin, and after saying the customary blessing, is on the point of digging into the viands set before him by headwaiters and costumed servants, you will threaten him with your whalebone rod, backed by the authority and the prestige of your imposing lexigraphic diplomas

you are to eat, Señor Hispano, only according to the uses and customs of the other islands I have inhabited: I am a grammarian, sir, and safeguard the purity of my native tongue with much more zeal than my own health, poring over my books night and day, studying the constitution of the Hispano so as to be able to cure him should he happen to fall ill: and my principal concern is watching over his meals and repasts, allowing him to partake of only those dishes that seem to me to be of native origin and forbidding him everything that is etymologically foreign to him.) (p. 166)[27]

Cervantes describes the cruelty of the doctor's attempt to make a capricious joke out of Sancho's newly acquired social position, all in the context of a general criticism of the Spanish aristocracy. Goytisolo reverses Cervantes's intention, rendering the doctor a positive character, a character who is the personification of Goytisolo's linguistic attempt to destroy sacred Spain. Julián's prohibition of any type of food that is the least bit foreign is filled with contradictions, given that much of what has been proscribed is typically Spanish (olives and saffron, for example). The logical consequence of Julián's orders is the ultimate irony of the passage: Sancho is prohibited not only Spanish foods but all food. He protests (p. 198), "Que me muero de hambre, y el negarme la comida, aunque le pese al señor gramático y él más me diga, antes será quitarme la vida que aumentármela" ("I am dying of hunger: and whatever Your Lordship the grammarian may say, keeping me from eating will shorten my life rather than lengthen it," p. 167). Goytisolo's outdoing of Cervantes's text consists of a search for the etymological roots of what has been considered "typically Spanish": "zanahorias" ("carrots"), "entremeses" ("hors d'oeuvres"), "berenjenas" ("eggplant"), "perdices" ("partridges"), all the Spanish culinary delights, are, in the last analysis, words whose signification has gone beyond a specific type of food and has come to signify the essence of Spain. Goytisolo's ironic word game ends in Julián's final utterance (p. 199), "y quítenme de ahí ese Guad-el-Kebir!" ("remove the Guad-el-Kebir as well!," p. 168).[28] In Goytisolo's scheme the geography of Spain is not Spanish. The letters in the name Guadalquivir (a river that has been the object of many poetic descriptions in Spanish literature) are arranged in such a way as to expose its Arabic origin.

Parody does not function in Goytisolo's work as an ethical, social, or even aesthetic judgment, the replacement of the negative with the positive, as is the case in satire. Goytisolo's parodies create new texts that penetrate the old texts and enter into a debate with them. The hostility within this debate is at the root of a tension between the two that is never completely resolved. Yet the open-ended, ambivalent nature of parody is incongruous with Goytisolo's attack on Spanish culture, a criticism that yearns to find the roots of the social order. The reader's encounter with such a subversive text engenders questions that remain unanswered: What new order does the author seek? What is the view of history that underlies the social critique? Is history a linear process of never-ending development, or is it a circular re-creation of deeply rooted myths?

In Goytisolo's literary development from *Juegos de manos* to this treasonous trilogy, there is evidence of a shift from an acceptance of the possibility of historical progress to a constant and static view of the human condition. Yet if Goytisolo advances the latter notion, how is he to accomplish his destruction of sacred Spain? The creation of a new mythology must emerge as the old is destroyed; the redeemed Don Julián will replace Seneca in Goytisolo's re-creation of his own culture. The paradoxical nature of Goytisolo's task, the simultaneous act of destruction and creation, is the root of a related dilemma in his role as author. Goytisolo engages in the destruction of writing while he writes. This contradiction inevitably leads to the annihilation of Goytisolo himself as writer. In the "Advertencia" that he appends to the text of *Don Julián*, he writes: "La presente obra se ha realizado con la participación póstuma o involuntaria de . . ." ("This work was written with the posthumous or unwitting collaboration of . . ."), which is followed by an alphabetical list of well-known figures of Spanish literature. This list reaffirms the ongoing process of creation–destruction that proceeds throughout the work. But as we read the names on the list, we become painfully aware that the most crucial author is missing—Juan Goytisolo.

5. From *Don Julián* to *Juan sin tierra*: Battle between the Selves

One of the most important consequences of intertextuality in literature is the always implicit, but sometimes explicit, commentary on the act of writing itself. Intertextuality creates, on the part of the authors, an intense consciousness of the activity of writing, of the artificiality or "literariness" of the product. In Goytisolo's texts, intertextuality is not only a tool to subvert and corrupt a literary tradition; it is a commentary on language. Insofar as Goytisolo's primary subject matter is writing, his texts have come to be known as self-reflective; that is, they show an awareness of their own process of development by exposing their own structures. Robert Alter defines the self-reflective novel as "a novel that systematically flaunts its own condition of artifice and that by so doing probes into the problematic relationship between real-seeming artifice and reality."[1] Intertextuality is itself an inherent feature of literary self-consciousness, for writers who make use of other texts within their own are ultimately aware of this dilemma: they must use language to describe language. The object becomes the subject.

The paradox inherent in the condition of the self-conscious writer is extremely important to the phenomenon of literary self-reflection, and it sheds a great deal of light on the tensions within Goytisolo's writing. According to Paul De Man, self-reflection is closely related to the problem of romantic irony.[2] The early nineteenth-century theoreticians of irony such as Friedrich Schlegel and Sören Kierkegaard were cognizant of an implicit self-commentary contained within an ironic discourse. By consciously disguising the signification of words, the ironist must always be aware of his or her own inauthenticity. The verbal denial that in effect negates the meaning of the words renders the writing particularly self-conscious. Charles Baudelaire, whose poetry was, in some ways, an outgrowth of that of the romantics, expressed a similar theory of irony. In reference to the French poet's essay "De l'essence du rire," De Man describes the phenomenon of duplication or *dédoublement* that occurs as a result of irony. The ironic writer necessarily distinguishes his or her real self from the self that appears in the artificial world of language. This differentiation involves a separation between the writer as an entity (self) in the world and the writer as a re-creation of that entity in language (the linguistic self).

> The relative disjunction not only occurs *by means of* language as a privileged category, but it transfers the self out of the empirical world into a world constituted out of, and in, language—a language that it finds in the world like one entity among others, but that remains unique in being the only entity by which it can differentiate itself from the world. Language thus conceived divides the subject into an empirical self, immersed in the world, and a self that becomes like a sign in its attempt at differentiation and self-definition.[3]

Thus within irony there is an implicit statement on the irreconcilability of the world of fiction and the real world. De Man points out that, for Schlegel, irony is a permanent "parabasis," or a permanent intrusion on the part of an author into his or her text. Such an intrusion exposes the artificiality of language and makes clear that the world of the text and the real world are in no way identical.

In the last two volumes of the trilogy, Goytisolo becomes increasingly aware of the phenomenon of self-consciousness in literature and incorporates this element into his own writing. The ensuing duplication of the self between an existential entity (a real person struggling to rid himself of oppressive forces) and a linguistic person (a *yo*, *tú*, or *nosotros* whose linguistic cosmos is self-sufficient and totally estranged from the world of reality) becomes evident on every page of *Juan sin tierra*. Goytisolo has never resolved this conflict, despite the resounding affirmation of victory in the final pages of the trilogy. The self-destructive dimension of *Don Julián*, which was hinted at in *Señas* and which saturates *Juan sin tierra* in the form of verbal suicide, remains in the last analysis a metaphor, a symbol of an act.[4]

Self-reflection in Don Julián

In the second volume of the trilogy, intertextuality involves an outward search for texts in an attempt to discover the author's inner self, an activity that is paradoxically self-reflective. The search for texts and for the self creates a situation in which the real world is set off against the world of artistic creation, reminiscent of the paradox of the ironist pointed out by De Man. Because Goytisolo shows that he is aware of this dilemma in a variety of ways, we are able to isolate the explicitly self-referential characteristics of his writing from implicitly self-conscious allusions to outside texts. In *Don Julián*, there is an interplay among and an ultimate unity of diverse elements: commentary and self-commentary, parody and self-parody, protagonist and author. The result of this self-critique is a tension between opposing forces: the new versus the old, creation versus destruction, life versus death.[5] In effect, the unity of these elements becomes the way in which Goytisolo can accomplish (or thinks he can accomplish) his task inside and outside language.

Goytisolo's self-conscious manner of writing is apparent from the start. The objects that will decorate the scene of Julián's invasion are described in a way that stresses their fictional and aesthetically functional nature. In the opening pages of *Don Julián*, the narrator breaks up the description of the "inhospitable land" with questions (p. 12)—"sol apático? : amotinadas nubes? : luz encabritada y violenta?" ("an apathetic sun: threatening thunderheads, blinding light rearing in fury?," p. 4)—as if he were discriminately gathering the objects (words) that he will need for his textual journey. On the following page (p. 13), direct reference is made to the creative process: "inventar, componer, mentir, fabular" ("invent, compose, lie, make up stories," p. 5); and later on the same page, "silencio, caballeros, se alza el telón : la representación empieza" ("silence please, ladies and gentlemen, the curtain is about to go up: the play is beginning!," p. 5). The comparison between a play and Goytisolo's own text leads to a further analogy between a play within a play and a text within a text. Comments such as these that reveal the process of literary creation are interspersed throughout the novel as readers become unable to remove themselves from the work of art. There is no pretense of achieving an accurate representation of reality. As in certain modern plays in which the suspension of disbelief is laid bare, Goytisolo makes it clear that the words in his text are (as are all words) representations of objects and not the objects themselves.

This self-consciousness—the frequent allusions to language in general and to the act of writing in particular—is a device that allows the reader to focus on the dominant tension throughout the work: destruction, on the one hand, and creation, on the other. All the words, images, and motifs that expose this process of creation and destruction also point to the text itself, that is, to Goytisolo's own act of writing. In this de facto unity of form and content, Julián's linguistic treason becomes the author's. A motif of verbal treason is constant: "la mezquina palabra despierta y ejecuta la implacable traición" (p. 126) ("the wretched word awakens and carries out the implacable act of treason," p. 106); "palabra liberada de secular servidumbre" (p. 125) ("the word freed after centuries in bondage," p. 106);[6] "los signos premonitorios se acumulan" (p. 137) ("the premonitory signs are multiplying," p. 114); "vehículo de la traición, hermosa lengua mía . . . idioma cruel y brusco" (pp. 195–96) ("oh my beautiful, noble language, the weapon of treason . . . [cruel and abrupt language]," p. 165). Behind all this linguistic destructiveness lies the act of literary creation, the construction of a text, an activity in which Julián becomes the text. If Julián is a literary creation, and if Julián's nature is to destroy, he must destroy himself and reproduce himself. This interplay between self-destruction and self-creation is the main tension that manifests itself in various ways throughout the work.

In the unity of these seemingly diverse elements (author, narrator, protagonist), we already perceive a doubling (*dédoublement*) of the self in Goytisolo.[7] The contamination, subversion, and ultimate destruction (the author's vindictive self) are placed in conjunction with the creation of a text, which is the manifestation of another self—Goytisolo as a linguistic entity (Julián). While Goytisolo intends these two selves to converge, the effect is the opposite. One witnesses instead a struggle between opposing forces: the real world versus the world of artistic creation, reality versus artifice. The struggle between these two forces is Goytisolo's quest for self.

It is significant that the search for authenticity (textual and real) is undertaken with a constant incorporation of outside texts within the main text. The exposure of the text's development through frequent references to the act of writing and to the actual text that is being written is tempered by the constant presence of outside texts. Julián is not only the embodiment of the text itself, he is also extracted from outside sources. Thus Goytisolo's textual self (the identification of the author with his own text) manifests itself through his use of that text as a mirror for others.

The relationship and integration of the elements of intertextuality and self-reflection are evident in several specific instances in *Don Julián*. The most striking example is the contrast between Alvaro and Julián. The many identities of both characters mark Goytisolo's ability to bring together the most diverse entities. Julián is transformed into an Arab warrior, an insect, a wolf, James Bond, and an asp, in addition to the changes in his name: Julián, Ulbán, Bulian, Urbano. Alvaro, in like manner, is Seneca, Unamuno, Don Alvaro Peranzules ("lawyer"), Alvarito, Little Red Riding Hood, as well as a reminder of the Alvaro in *Señas*. Yet the most crucial identity change in both characters is their ability to become one another. At times Alvaro and Julián are presented as separate beings who display opposing characteristics. Don Alvaro Peranzules, for example, is the object of satire for his pedantic evocations of Spanish culture: he offers the narrator some Spanish excrement and tells him to take in the wonderful aroma. Julián, on the other hand, constantly shows his disgust for everything Spanish: he attempts to destroy all that Alvaro symbolizes—Spanish customs, Spanish literature, Catholicism, even the geography of Spain. Yet, in other situations,

Julián and Alvaro appear as a single entity with two sides. In these cases, there is a recurrent seduction of Alvaro by Julián in which Alvaro becomes Julián, and Julián becomes Alvaro.

The self-reflective nature of this dialectical unity of opposites (Alvaro and Julián) is apparent in the fact that both characters are embodiments of Goytisolo's previous writing. Alvaro is the protagonist of *Señas*, and Julián's destructive and vindictive spirit is the theme of *Don Julián*. But at the same time, these two separate but equal entities reflect a literary world outside the text. The dual nature of the text's attempt at self-definition is revealed in the recurring scenes of seduction. In one of these instances, Don Alvaro's daughter assumes the identity of Queen Isabella. As she is about to go to bed, a song by the Rolling Stones, "Time Is on My Side," is heard. She attempts to recite her prayers à la Santa Teresa (pp. 163–64)—"amarte, amarte dueño y señor mío, es mi delirio constante! : estoy enferma de amor pero no quiero curarme jamás" ("loving you, loving you, my lord and master, is my constant delirious dream: I am sick of love, but do not want to be cured," p. 138), but she remains unable to pray. She cannot keep herself from tapping her feet and swaying her body to the music as the beat of the song overtakes her. She slowly takes off her dress as in a striptease. The way in which the sound waves multiply, erupt, and penetrate intensifies as she becomes uncontrollably aroused by her own body (p. 164): "descubre la insólita perfección de sus piernas" ("revealing the incomparable perfection of her limbs," p. 138). The scene culminates in an act of autoflagellation, a type of self-seduction in which Goytisolo suggests the presence of Julián in the form of the Rolling Stones. The musicians of the counterculture (Julián) have entered her body, forcing her to commit this disgusting yet tremendously satisfying deed. In an act of sadomasochism, Don Alvaro's daughter (the queen) has taken on the qualities of Julián, and in like manner, all the extratextual entities (Queen Isabella, Santa Teresa, the Rolling Stones) appear within the text as elements of self-reflection.

There is further evidence of a convergence of intertextuality and self-reflection in the re-creation and repetition of the fairy tale of Little Red Riding Hood, which is itself an intertextual feature (an outside text within the main text). The story is read to Alvarito in a strange mixture of fairy-tale fantasy and childhood nightmare. As the servant reads the story, Alvarito's imagination wanders when he recalls a similar story (also told by the servant) in which a big man with a bushy mustache who looks like an Arab drives out a woman with whom he has been living, whipping her with his belt. The woman has a demented child on whom the man urinates to show his disdain for the woman. The similarities between this cruel man and the wolf in "Little Red Riding Hood" lead to a further association with Julián. Alvarito's anxiety as he listens to both stories and his utter fascination at their perversity are reminiscent of the emotions experienced by Don Alvaro's daughter and reappear in other situations throughout the novel. Such perverse delight in all that opposes established cultural values (the sanctity of virginity, the negation of the body, and the repression of sexuality) creates a bond between Alvaro and Julián as they become one with the text.

In the final part of *Don Julián*, there is a re-creation of the "Little Red Riding Hood" story. In this instance, Alvarito actually becomes a male Red Riding Hood ("Caperucito Rojo"), and Julián is transformed into the wolf. The re-creation of the story and the insertion of elements of contemporary society "Social Assistance," urban renewal or "superurbanización," the recipe for the cakes) are parodic elements common to other rewritings of texts. But this time, Goytisolo adds elements that go beyond the parodies of other texts and into the realm of self-parody. The final version of the "Little Red Riding Hood" story is a rewriting of a rewriting.[8] The characters of the first version are all present again, but in the second version, these characters are synthesized into two opposing forces that ultimately become one. All the situations of the first are evident in the second, but again with a difference. In the second version, there is a symbiotic relationship between the two characters; the descriptions of Julián's cruelty toward the innocent Alvaro make it painfully clear that Alvaro depends on Julián and vice versa. Alvarito always returns to his torturer, and in like manner, the beatings and flagellations revitalize Julián. Julián sees himself in Alvarito; the phrase "tú mismo un cuarto de siglo atrás" ("you yourself a quarter of a century ago") reappears several times. The scene ends as Alvarito chooses to hang himself rather than allow his mother to be raped by Julián (p. 230): "y, tal el halcón al acecho, apuras la brevedad del milagro : abrazándote a él : serpiente troglodita, flagelador hircino . . . monstruo no, ni bifronte, ni hermes : tú mismo al fin, único, en el fondo de tu animalidad herida" ("and like the falcon diving on its prey, you will hasten the miracle: pressing him to your bosom: a troglodytic reptile, a hircine flagellator . . . not a monster, or a two-faced creature, or a Janus: you yourself at last, become one and indivisible, in the very depths of your tortured animality," p. 195). In this last scene, the characters merge into one ("tú mismo al fin, único") by way of a self-inflicted death. There is also a suggestion of verbal suicide ("apuras la brevedad del milagro") in which the *tú* refers not only to Alvaro–Julián but also to Julián–Goytisolo. The subject of the verb *apurar* refers to the author in his attempt to synthesize his act of writing with an act of sexual perversion.

The theme of sex-as-death is closely connected to the self-referential structure of *Don Julián*. The constant presence of the *serpiente* ("serpent") or *culebra* ("snake") is a motif that can be found in the medieval legends about Count Julián. In the old ballads, Count Julián suffers penance for his crime by being devoured by a snake. The illicit sexual relationship between Count Julián's daughter and Don Rodrigo is made explicit as Goytisolo turns the snake into a phallus. The snake is the most important vehicle by which Julián will subvert, invade, seduce, and infect all that is abhorrent to him, yet it is also the link between opposing forces: Spain–Africa, Alvaro–Julián, victim–seducer. In the opening pages, Goytisolo writes (p. 13): "el mar convertido en lago, unido tú a la otra orilla como el feto al útero sangriento de la madre, el cordón umbilical entre los dos como una larga y ondulante serpentina" ("the sea having turned into a lake, links you to the other shore, as the fetus is tied to the mother's blood-engorged womb, the umbilical cord between them coiling like a long, sinuous strip of *serpentin*," p. 4). The serpentine nature of the umbilical cord and the bloody uterus reveal the life-giving qualities of this *serpiente*, which are rein-forced as the work continues. The snake, however, does not function as a harmonious mediator between opposing elements. Like the text itself, it nourishes the conflict by bringing on death; it is a creative destroyer. The killer-snake and the procreating phallus reveal the unity of the opposing elements of the text. In part 1 the description of an Arab's musical enticement of a cobra ends in Mrs. Putifar's slow death from the snake's poisonous bite. In part 2 a scorpion, another phallic symbol, is observed by Alvarito in an elementary-school science class. The scorpion's pincers become erect, and it seizes a defenseless grasshopper, planting its poisonous dart inside the victim (p. 93).

The close relationship between sex and death is akin to Goytisolo's dual concept of writing as a form of verbal suicide and as an act of procreation. Goytisolo rewrites his own renditions of the events in the text, thereby corrupting the previous significa-tion of his own words. In this undertaking, words die and are re-created as they reappear in different situations. Each time the verbal assassination comes to a climax, there is a linguistic rejuvenation. By constantly regenerating itself, the destruction never seems to end. In the act of writing, Goytisolo seems to have found the self-perpetuating crime for which the marquis de Sade yearned in the novel's epigraph.

That quotation from Sade's *Les cent vingt journées* sheds light on the relationship between texts in Goytisolo, for Sade is present within Goytisolo in three separate ways: Sade's text stands appended to and inside of *Don Julián*; it is a mirror of *Don Julián* in its creative perversity; and it repeats itself. These three categories underscore the concept of the self in Goytisolo. Besides searching for his identity through the creation of a text (through his own ordering of language), Goytisolo also undertakes his search through a reading and assimilation of other texts that stand in opposition to and in alliance with his own. Goytisolo reaches outward in order to turn inward. The subversion, corruption, contamination, and destruction of sacred Spain is in reality self-subversion, self-corruption, self-contamination, and self-destruction.

Juan sin tierra *and the Intertextual Self*

Goytisolo ends the second volume of the trilogy with a warning (p. 240): "la invasión recomenzará" ("the invasion will begin all over again," p. 204). Besides being a commentary on the never-ending process of self-destruction and self-regeneration that is central to *Don Julián*, these words also refer to the next phase of the process: *Juan sin tierra*. Goytisolo sees this third and last volume as the end of a cycle of linguistic infection that began with *Señas de identidad*.[9] As this cycle comes to an end, the reader recalls its beginning through the allusions to *Señas*. The letter from Casilda Goytisolo, the Cuban slave and mistress of one of the author's ancestors, is reproduced in its entirety in *Juan sin tierra* (pp. 313–14) as it was in the first edition of *Señas*.[10] Immediately after the closing of the letter, which in the novel is signed Casilda Mendiola, Goytisolo comments on its personal effects (p. 314): "grito de dolor / fuente secreta del proceso liberador de tu pluma / razón oculta de tu desvío moral y artístico, social, religioso, sexual" ("a cry of pain / the secret source of your pen's process of liberation / the hidden reason for your moral, artistic, social, religious, sexual deviation," p. 263). The reaction that follows (pp. 314–16) continues the search for the origins of Goytisolo's disaffection. In like manner, "diez años atrás" ("ten years before") refers to the commencement of the trilogy. But Goytisolo has not left off at the exact spot at which he began. The long and arduous process has made for significant changes in his conception of writing. The attempt to infiltrate the mother country with the contaminating forces of language has become stronger, and the self-consciousness of this enterprise has completely overcome the elements of historical and social realism implicit in *Señas.*[11]

Goytisolo has stated that the differences between *Don Julián* and *Juan sin tierra* revolve around the presence of a "centripetal force" in the final volume that establishes the act of writing as the central organizing principle. In *Don Julián*, on the other hand, there is a "centrifugal force"[12] based on the classical unities of time and place as well as on the remarkable coherence of motifs: the snake, Seneca, and the frequent seductions that are all in some way connected to the main theme of cultural and linguistic corruption. Severo Sarduy discusses the differences in terms of the presence of characters in *Don Julián* and their disappearance in *Juan sin tierra* where they become purely linguistic entities by taking the form of pronouns. In his characteristically baroque prose, Sarduy writes that in *Juan sin tierra* characters dissolve as in a dream, for everything in the novel, things as well as beings, refers to itself as "I." Pronouns do not designate real objects or people; they only function syntactically.[13] The action in *Don Julián* takes place in Tangier, while in *Juan sin tierra* it occurs within the text.

The shift from *Don Julián* to *Juan sin tierra* illustrates the growing importance of language as theme from the commencement of the trilogy to the end. At the beginning of the cycle (*Señas*), Goytisolo is concerned with the re-creation and manipulation of outside texts. In this phase the outside text has its own identity and can exist both inside and outside Goytisolo's text. The focal point of *Don Julián* changes as certain outside texts become reflections of the text that is being written (a phenomenon that suggests a self-conscious form of intertextuality). The transition to *Juan sin tierra* involves the continuation of the self-reflective usage of outside texts as one aspect of an all-encompassing element—the commentary on the act of writing. The most important text of *Juan sin tierra* is language itself.

Goytisolo's ongoing commentary on language takes shape in the first section of *Juan sin tierra* (pp. 11–15) and continues in much the same vein throughout the work. In these introductory pages someone (a second-person narrator) is gazing at a photograph of a black woman on a record jacket on which the words, "La reina del ritmo" ("the queen of rhythm") appear. The queen's alluring body is described in great detail as the speaker (the *tú*) compares the waves or ruffles in the fabric she wears to the sea swells of an Antillean hurricane that is about to destroy a village. But, says the *tú*-narrator, who continues to stare (p. 12), "la ola no avanza y estalla y la instantánea del fotógrafo la aquieta, remansa e inmoviliza" ("but the wave does not in fact advance toward the shore and break, and the photographer's snapshot calms it, arrests it, immobilizes it," p. 3). A photographer's power to halt the forces of nature is associated with an author's ability to alter reality by arranging and reorganizing the language that describes it. As the *tú* focuses its attention on the midsection of the woman, it describes a part of her body that cannot be seen in the photo—the buttocks (pp. 12–13): "la línea Maginot del corsé sugiere más bien la hipótesis de dos lomas de forma ovoide y superficie turgente, cuyo saliente extremo se mantiene en inverosímil y precario equilibrio" ("the Maginot line of the corset suggests, rather, the hypothesis of two hills, oval in shape and with a swollen surface, the salient point of which maintains itself in improbable, precarious balance," p. 3). The *tú* is not only able to control nature; it can also see what cannot be seen in reality—the posterior of a woman who has been photographed from the front. The description of this regal rump continues (p. 13): "cordilleras, vaguadas, cerros, pasos, colinas, desfiladeros? : no : la geometría lo expresará mejor : círculos, discos, esferas, orbes que invitan al estudio y observación, a las especulaciones exquisitas del perito agrimensor que sueña en poseer para sí todo el fausto y grandeza del espectacular hemiciclo" ("cordilleras, water courses, ridges, passes, hills, gorges? no, geometry will express it better: circles, disks, spheres, globes that invite the study and observation, the discriminating speculations of the expert land surveyor who dreams of possessing for himself all the splendor and grandeur of the spectacular hemicycle," p. 4). The *tú* is engaged in the distortion of reality for artistic ends. The preference for geometry over geography is not only suggestive of a cubist painting that obscures reality by focusing on the geometric shapes of objects; it also exposes the artificiality of the words that describe the photograph. The distortion and artificiality are enhanced since these words are figures of a figure (the photo) of a human being. Later the *tú* actually enters the photo (p. 14): "dando la vuelta, a fin de sortearla te adentrarás en él" ("and turning away, in order to walk behind her, you will venture into the plantation yard," p. 4). This act, the penetration of the photograph, establishes the point of departure for the rest of the novel. The *tú* who observes and describes, who transforms what it sees into language, enters the false world of artistic creation. The *tú* is thus the vehicle with which Goytisolo draws together three important factors: protagonist, narrator, and author. The protagonist is in effect the narrator who is in turn a writer, an observer whose existential concerns are those of Goytisolo. The *tú* is the bond between the real self and the written self within Goytisolo.[14]

Every chapter subdivision of *Juan sin tierra* draws the reader's attention to the act of literary creation by direct comments or by reflections on the text's development. Unlike *Don Julián*, in which explicit commentaries on writing are scarce, references to the pen and to the hand that wields it abound in the last volume of the trilogy. The first of the book's seven chapters, for example, intersperses segments of a sermon on the vices and inferiority of the black slaves of a sugar plantation with separate segments on the text that is being written. The voice of the *tú* always seems to be at the helm of this process: "míralos bien . . . te interrumpirás unos segundos a fin de completar el decorado" (p. 15) ("take a good look at them . . . you will interrupt your train of thought for a few seconds in order to sketch in the decor," p. 6); "dividirás la imaginaria escena en dos partes : dicho mejor : en dos bloques opuestos de palabras" (p. 30) ("you will divide the imaginary scene into two parts: or better put: into two opposed blocks of words," p. 20); "interrupción, oquedad, silencio : como cuando dejas de escribir" (p. 32) ("interruption, emptiness, silence: as when you stop writing," p. 22); "seguirás sin interrumpirte" (p. 34) ("you will go on without a pause," p. 24); "acometerás la descripción de un paisaje alpino" (p. 38) ("you will attempt to describe an Alpine landscape," p. 28); "hablará el capellán" (p. 47) ("the chaplain will begin to speak," p. 36); "interrumpirás la lectura de documentos" (p. 51) ("you will break off your reading of the documents," p. 39). The motif of literary creation is evident not only in this chapter but also throughout the work.

While the theme of writing remains the unifying principle, it is by no means the only ingredient of this seemingly incoherent work. The decadence of Spanish culture, censorship, and the pathological denial of the body are all thematic factors in *Juan sin tierra* as they are in *Don Julián*. Yet writing as theme is an indispensable feature without which the secondary themes would have absolutely no place in Goytisolo's system of linguistic corruption and contagion. In like manner, the presence of outside texts in *Juan sin tierra* is every bit as strong as it is in *Don Julián*. In the last book in the trilogy, however, the intertextual aspects are subsumed into a broader category: the reflection on writing and language in general and on the particular text that is being written—*Juan sin tierra*. Thus the final stage of Goytisolo's trilogy is itself one of the most crucial intertexts.

The changing nature of intertextuality for Goytisolo is apparent in the diminishing importance that he attaches to the Spanish literary tradition in *Juan sin tierra*. Goytisolo has pointed out that intertextual relationships in *Juan sin tierra* are not limited to Spanish literature but extend to other languages and cultures as well.[15] The book's title itself testifies to Goytisolo's wish to traverse the Pyrenees. The name *Juan sin tierra* or "Juan sin Tierra" (p. 89) is taken from a volume of poetry titled *Jean sans terre* by the Alsatian poet Ivan Goll. Goytisolo's novelistic entity, Juan sin Tierra, assumes all the traits of the character in Goll's poem. In the preface to the Spanish translation of *Jean sans terre*, Goll describes his creation as a legendary character who symbolizes modern man and the modern poet. He has no cultural roots in any nation and travels from "continent to continent, from society to society, and from star to star."[16] The three most salient literary and historical figures who appear in the final volume of the trilogy are equally nomadic and cross-cultural: Anselm Turmeda (who did not consider himself a Spaniard), Père de Foucauld, and T. E. Lawrence (of Arabia). Goytisolo reaches out beyond his earlier territorial limits to find the material for this novel. It is ironic that this outward striving is in reality Goytisolo's inward search for his linguistic and cultural identity, for in these three writers, Goytisolo sees his own reflection.

The differences in the spiritual concerns among Turmeda, Foucauld, and Lawrence, not to mention their disparities in time and place, are superficial in Goytisolo's eyes. In *Juan sin tierra* all three are bound by a fascination with Arab culture and civilization. Through the use of the texts by and about these figures, Goytisolo is able to continue the dialectical interplay between Europe and North Africa, between Christianity and Islam, that he had initiated in *Don Julián*. In *Juan sin tierra*, however, the specific employment of these three figures is integral to the self-reflective structure of the work.

Turmeda, Foucauld, and Lawrence are not grasped by Goytisolo from the outside and placed in strategic points within the text as was Seneca in *Don Julián*; they seem to come from within Goytisolo as expressions of his own linguistic designs.[17] At one point Goytisolo refers to all three figures as embodiments of his own desires:

> el desierto te invita de nuevo, vasto y tenaz como tu deseo, y te internarás en la maciza configuración de su implacable pecho cobrizo : brazos montuosos amurallarán la línea del horizonte, aislándote misericordiosamente del mundo fértil y hostil : paso a paso, sobre el escudo de su abdomen liso, alcanzarás el oasis más próximo gracias al fino instinto de los meharís : Anselm Turmeda, Père de Foucauld, Lawrence de Arabia? : entre los tuyos al fin (p. 87)

> (the desert beckons to you once again, as vast and stubborn as your desire, and you will penetrate the dense configuration of its implacable, copper-colored breast: mountainous arms will wall off the line of the horizon, mercifully isolating you from the fertile and hostile world:

striding step by step across the sheath of its smooth abdomen, you will reach the next oasis thanks to the subtle instinct of the Meharis: Anselm Turmeda, Father Foucauld, Lawrence of Arabia?: amid those of your kind at last. (p. 72)

For all their seeming dissimilarity, these personages are united in *Juan sin tierra* by their spiritual attraction to the desert, a passion that is shared by Goytisolo.

An indication of the self-reflective nature of intertextuality in *Juan sin tierra* is the presence of T. E. Lawrence. The similarities between Lawrence's life and Goytisolo's are clear: both wish to become Arabs, Lawrence in reality and Goytisolo through his writing. Both men seek the rejuvenation and revitalization of Arab culture. Yet Lawrence's historical attempt to render the Arab renaissance a reality becomes pure artifice in Goytisolo's text. The self-styled British-Arab who fought against the Turks alongside King Faisal during World War I compiled his bellicose memoirs in *Seven Pillars of Wisdom*, a book that Goytisolo's author-narrator keeps with him at all times (p. 123).[18] Goytisolo re-creates the battle scenes of *Seven Pillars* as he alludes to the specific geographic locations of the battles as well as to the cities in which Lawrence's military strategy was mapped out: Damascus, Baghdad, and Istanbul (pp. 97–100, 123–26). It is significant that these scenes are not extracted from *Seven Pillars* and simply interpolated in their entirety among the situations created by Goytisolo. Rather, the words of Lawrence and those of Goytisolo mesh into one voice. As the author-narrator rids himself of his "importuna personalidad inglesa" (p. 123) ("irksome English personality," p. 104), Goytisolo evokes Lawrence's arduous search for Arab unity and freedom. This noble search and his nomadic existence are described in several instances. The *tú* speaks of "blowing up Ottoman locomotives" (p. 98) and of "making camp just outside Qalaat Simáan" (p. 123) so that he may attack the next day. He also stresses the determination to "avenge the affront suffered in Deráa" (p. 161). Yet the warlike nature of Lawrence's activity has been transformed into a different form of subversion in *Juan sin tierra*—the act of writing:

pero renunciando provisionalmente a los lauros de la campaña para orquestar la gama de tus emociones en una incierta, experimental sinfonía, artística y moralmente atonal : atentados, pillajes, razzias, descarrilamientos servirán en adelante de pretexto a los juegos sutiles de la escritura . . . recreando tu mundo en la página en blanco : la liberación de Damasco no apremia y, escalando a la testa del cuerpo islámico, te demorarás una vez más a tus anchas en la frondosidad de los babilonios pensiles : su enmarañado boscaje celará el fervor de tu entrega, desde sus guías recias e hirsutas atalayarás la greña que cubre el áspero y rugoso mentón! : panorama más tentador no pudiera ofrecerte el diablo, y el vértigo de la pasión te fulmina : en el reposo del guerrero hallarás el octavo pilar de la sabiduría : ciegamente te precipitarás en el ardiente volcán de los labios (pp. 125–27)

(renouncing for the moment, however, the laurels of a successful campaign in order to orchestrate the full range of your emotions in a hesitant, experimental symphony, artistically and morally atonal: attacks, pillage, raids, derailments will henceforth serve you as a pretext for the subtle games of literary composition . . . recreating your world on the blank page: the liberation of Damascus is not pressing, and ascending to the head of the Islamic body, you will tarry once again in the luxuriant foliage of the hanging gardens of Babylon: their tangled vegetation will conceal the fervor of your surrender: from the stiff, bristling hairs of the handlebar mustache you will observe the matted hair that covers the rough and rugged chin! the devil himself could not offer you a more tempting prospect and the vertigo of passion assails you like a bolt of lightening: in the warrior's repose you will find the eighth pillar of wisdom: you will blindly hurl yourself into the burning-hot volcano of the lips) (pp. 106–7)

Goytisolo demonstrates an awareness of Lawrence's utter failure to actually accomplish his military and political goals while he praises the glories of achieving these goals in writing. Lawrence is successful only with the aid of Goytisolo's text, as *Seven Pillars* blends with *Juan sin tierra*. The "eighth pillar of wisdom," the title of a subchapter, is, therefore, *Juan sin tierra*: the ultimate step beyond the seventh pillar into a world where virtually everything is possible—the world of literary creation.

Unlike Lawrence, who is better known as a historical figure than as a writer, Anselm Turmeda (1352–1432) was primarily a man of letters. However, he shares with Lawrence the zeal and fascination for Arab culture, as evidenced in his conversion from

Christianity to Islam around 1386. An ordained Franciscan, Turmeda renounced his faith and subsequently traveled to Tunis where he spent the rest of his life as a Muslim and was known as Aleaclum Abdalla. This Majorcan renegade, as he is affectionately called by Goytisolo,[19] wrote several works, the most famous of which, *Disputa de l'ase contra frare Encelm Turmeda sobre la natura y noblessa dels animals (The Ass's Debate against Friar Anselm Turmeda on the Nature and Nobility of Animals)*,[20] appears in a modified form in *Juan sin tierra*. Besides being inspired by Turmeda's defiant act of conversion, Goytisolo also admires the *Disputa*'s skepticism, satire, and subversion of established Christian beliefs. The *Disputa* consists of a debate between Turmeda and an ass (a representative of the animal kingdom) on the superiority of animals over human beings. Every argument defending man's superiority is ingeniously destroyed by the ass. Fray Anselm states, for example, that men have much scientific knowledge and are able to govern themselves. The ass responds by citing the perfect organization and harmony that exist among bees and locusts.[21] Goytisolo makes use of these arguments in *Juan sin tierra* when he expresses man's bond with animals, especially in bodily functions. In one section of *Juan sin tierra* Turmeda appears as a character and, along with the author-narrator, contemplates an open sewer (p. 171): "el propio Ibn Turmeda en persona contemplará la escena contigo . . . asidos con familiaridad de la mano, planearéis con cirujana delectación nuevas traiciones y felonías, insidias y partidas serranas : hermanados los dos en la execrada abjuración . . . sin inepto pudo quant au genre de jouissance" ("and Ibn Turmeda in person will contemplate the scene with you . . . clasping each other's hands in affectionate intimacy, you will plot, with the glow of pleasure of surgeons, new acts of betrayal, treacherous crimes, traps, and disloyalties: the two of you fraternally united in the accursed abjuration . . . with no stupid sense of shame," p. 144). At another point Turmeda and the *tú* are joined by a *nosotros* who pays homage to the animal kingdom:

no mantenemos ningún criterio elitista con respecto a la flora y la fauna : auspiciamos por igual todas las especies vegetales y animales, incluso aquellas que, con egocentrismo aberrante, los hombres del pasado decretaban nocivas e inútiles : ahora chinches, piojos y demás parásitos viven apaciblemente de nosotros del mismo modo que nosotros vivimos de los bienes fungibles del suelo : siguiendo las pautas del venerable Ibn Turmeda, hemos democratizado la escala animal y no nos tomamos, como antes solíamos, por reyes y señores de nadie : las especies tenidas por viles y abyectas florecen sin trabas en nuestra sociedad (p. 249)

(we apply no elitist criterion to the various flora and fauna: we give equal opportunities to all vegetable and animal species, including those which, with errant egocentrism, the men of the past deemed noxious and useless: bedbugs, lice, and other parasites now live peaceably off us as we live off the fungible goods of the soil: following the precepts of the venerable Ibn Turmeda, we have democratized the animal hierarchy and no longer take ourselves to be, as we once did, the lords and masters of anyone: those species once considered vile and abject flourish without impediment in our society) (p. 206)

In Turmeda's text Fray Anselm argues that man's superiority to animals is justified by the fact that the former eats the latter. The ass responds that the reverse is also true and cites examples of a variety of parasites (lice, fleas, bedbugs) that feed on human flesh.[22] Turmeda's irony is basically ethical; he points out the vanity of man and affirms natural equality under God (or Allah). Yet Turmeda's moral intention is rendered ambiguous with Goytisolo's treatment of the *Disputa*. The irony of the Muslim changes when it is placed in conjunction with that of Goytisolo. Turmeda appears as a modern-day naturalist who, along with Goytisolo, extols the truly democratic nature of the animal world, a society in which all living things are equal and subservient to no single entity.

While Turmeda and Lawrence are Goytisolo's allies in his linguistic battle of contagion, Charles de Foucauld (1858–1916) is a figure whose affinity with Goytisolo is not as clear. A Trappist monk who died in martyrdom at the hands of an Arab chieftain, Foucauld had spiritual concerns that were by no means akin to those of Goytisolo. Yet this contradiction creates a tight bond between them. In two consecutive subchapters, "El falo [phallus] de Ghardaia" (a playful allusion to "el faro de Ghardaia" where Foucauld spent some time) and "Tras las huellas del Père de Foucauld," Goytisolo re-creates the religious Frenchman's journeys to Africa that are described in his letters to his cousin, Madeleine de Bondy. The monk's thirst for physical pain and martyrdom and his strange fascination for the desert make up the bulk of the subject matter of the letters.[23] These themes appear in *Juan sin tierra* as manifestations of an important element in Goytisolo's own writing—the desire to kill the religious fervor that the Spanish author felt as a child. The last volume of the trilogy contains a reenactment of the verbal suicide that was rampant in *Don Julián*. Foucauld is in effect Alvarito, another victim of the forces of corruption and contagion.

In "El falo de Ghardaia" (pp. 149–61), Goytisolo begins the subversion of the monk's religious zeal by reliving "los delirious y raptos del Révérend Père de Foucauld" (p. 150) ("the fits of delirium and ecstasy of the Reverend Père de Foucauld," p. 125). Goytisolo extracts a fragment of one of Foucauld's letters and inserts it into his text (pp. 150–51): "cette Afrique, ces missions d'infidèles appellent tellement la sainteté que seule obtiendra leur conversion . . . il faut passer par le désert, et y séjourner pour recevoir la grace de Dieu . . . désir d'aller jusqu'au bout dans l'amour et dans le don : et d'en tirer toutes les conséquences : je crois que c'est ma vocation : de descendre : pauvre, méprisé, abject : soif de mener enfin la vie que je cherche" ("this Africa, these missions ministering to infidels call forth so irresistibly the saintliness that will be the means of converting them . . . one must pass by way of the desert, and tarry there in order to receive God's grace . . . the desire to experience love and the giving of oneself to the limit: and to learn every lesson that they teach: I believe that that is my vocation: to descend: poor, scorned, abject: a thirst to lead at last the life I am seeking," p. 126).[24] In the subsequent pages Goytisolo gives Foucauld precisely what he asks for—flagellation—and makes it clear that this punishment will be performed through the act of writing (p. 152): "permanecerás al acecho de sus [Foucauld's] palabras (ave rapaz tú mismo) aguardando el placer clandestino que el correr de la pluma (del sexo) creará en el espacio textual" ("you will lie in ambush awaiting his words (a bird of prey yourself), looking forward to the clandestine pleasure that the flow of the pen (of the sex organ) will create in the space of the text," pp. 126–27). As the slow process of self-destruction continues, Goytisolo enlists the aid of his spiritual and textual allies—Turmeda, Lawrence, and Ebeh, the Arab who murdered Foucauld in Tamanrasset. All these figures are at the author's service as Goytisolo exposes the artificiality of his own activity (p. 159): "mudan las sombras errantes en vuestra imprescindble horma huera, y hábilmente podrás jugar con los signos sin que el lector ingenuo lo advierta : sumergíendole en un mundo fluyente, sometido a un proceso continuo de destrucción : distribuyendo entre tus egos dispersos los distintos papeles del coro y orquestándolos a continuación conforme al vuelo inspirado de la batuta : el leve correr de la pluma en el espacio rectangular de la página" ("the wandering shades change in your indispensable hollow mold, and you will be able to play sly games with the signs without the ingenuous reader's noticing: submerging him in a world in flux, the object of a continuous process of destruction: distributing among your shattered egos the various roles of the chorus and continually orchestrating them in accordance with the inspired movements of your baton: the swift flight of the pen over the rectangular space of the page," p. 133). As the ink flows onto the page, Foucauld (a mirror of Goytisolo's once religious self) is violently effaced.

Flagellation is transformed into murder as the treatment of Foucauld continues in the next subchapter, "Tras las huellas del Père de Foucauld" (pp. 165–68). Both victim and assassin seem to receive a great deal of pleasure from the perpetration of the crime. The "ansiado maritio de Tamanrasset" (p. 165) ("the longed-for martyrdom of Tamanrasset," p. 138) and the perverse joy at being the one who implements pain—"el vivísimo dolor de los golpes te inundará suavemente de dicha" ("the agony of the blows slowly fills you with joy")—are described in detail as the *tú* follows Foucauld's trajectory through the Sahara. Yet at the very last moment of the monk's life, the *tú* changes identities and becomes Foucauld himself. As he remains on his knees, with a rope around his neck and his hands tied behind his back, he comments on his own execution (p. 168): "el egoísta y estéril placer del martirio : tu mísera gloria usurpada" ("the selfish, sterile pleasure of martyrdom: your wretched usurped glory," p. 140). When the executioner pulls the trigger, the victim catches a glimpse of the inscription on his own grave (p. 168): "Les restes du serviteur de Dieu Charles de Jésus Vicompte [*sic*] de Foucauld (1858–1916)." The distance between Foucauld, on the one hand, and Turmeda and Lawrence, on the other, is only superficial: they are, in the last analysis, opposing elements that become one within the borders of *Juan sin tierra*.

While these textual allies of *Juan sin tierra*, the literary reflections of Goytisolo's novel, appear in the form of explicit references, imitations, and citations, the presence of other texts is intuited by the specific concerns of the author-narrator. Like Américo Castro's concept of history in *Don Julián*, the presence of Octavio Paz is felt throughout *Juan sin tierra* in the form of commentaries on writing and language. The two works by Paz that stand out most clearly in the last volume of the trilogy are *Conjunciones y disyunciones (Conjunctions and Disjunctions)* and *El mono gramático (The Ape-Grammarian)*.[25] In both of these works, Paz expresses the affinity between the act of writing and sexual play, between the text and the body. The specific treatment of this theme illustrates the bond between Paz's concept of writing and that of Goytisolo. Paz's works are, therefore, intertexts within the final phase of the trilogy. The first of three epigraphs of *Juan sin tierra* is a quotation from *Conjunciones* (p. 29): "La cara se alejó del culo" ("The face drew farther and farther away from the ass"). The dialectical relationship between the face and the anus is a central motif in Goytisolo's work. In like manner, the appearance of King Kong and other simians in *Juan sin tierra* is not only an allusion to the Hollywood film but also to the protagonist of Paz's *El mono gramático*.

Like Goytisolo, Paz bridges the gap between fiction and discourse on fiction with a variety of poetic devices within an essayistic prose *(Conjunciones)* and with the philosophical commentaries within a narrative *(El mono gramático)*. Furthermore, Paz affirms the inherently erotic nature of writing. His theories do not laud the virtues of pornography (even though several scenes in *El mono gramático* could be considered pornographic); rather, Paz argues that writing is itself a primitively pleasurable act, regardless of the subject matter. Luis de Góngora and Francisco de Quevedo (two of Goytisolo's most revered poets) are seen by Paz as writers who are intensely aware of the erotic quality of their craft and whose metaphors underline the vital relationship between the body and the text. Although the language of Góngora and Quevedo seems highly artificial, submits Paz, these poets give us the sensation of a live body. They were fully aware of the language–body relationship in spite of the seventeenth century's attempts to forget it (p. 20). Paz's *Mono* is a further manifestation of this notion. Throughout the work the protagonist is on a voyage with no end, a trip that he invents while he travels. In many instances we find reflections on this journey and on the path that leads nowhere. The road traveled, says the speaker at one point, is a road of writing, and writing is curiously like the body in that both are always unattainable; they resist any attempt at definition or possession. The sense of meaning in writing, he goes on, always appears as an end, but this end ceases to exist the moment we arrive. "The body is always beyond the body," for when we touch it, it divides itself (as does a text when we read it) into sensations (p. 123).

Goytisolo's writing is a testimonial to these notions of language. Paz's concepts appear in a variety of forms in *Juan sin tierra* as well as in Goytisolo's book of essays titled *Disidencias* in which he explicitly states his admiration for Paz's writing, specifically *Conjunciones* and *Mono*. According to Goytisolo, these works challenge the fundamental doctrine of the Judeo-Christian tradition, especially with regard to the body. Goytisolo affirms that the body has been a constant victim of theological abstractions, the tools of bourgeois exploitation (p. 176).[26] These rational and theological abstractions are the main objects of Goytisolo's fury in the final volume of the trilogy.[27]

Self-creation, Sexuality, and Filth

In recent years an ongoing discussion has arisen concerning the link between sexual activity and writing. Paz is by no means the only writer who has dealt with this issue. Edward W. Said, whose interest in Freud is evident in his *Beginnings,* writes: "The central symbol for the modern producing writer depicts the physical transfer of an image from man's sexual-procreative life to his artistic one. A writer's writing, in other words, is the result of daring to apply sexual energy or attention to the act of writing. The image of the writer . . . is . . . an intensified confusion of production with product, of career with text, of textuality with sexuality, of image with career."[28] Goytisolo is another writer who has shown interest in this problem. In fact he is consciously engaged in the same activity that Said and Paz describe. But while Said intrudes into Goytisolo's texts indirectly, Paz manifests a constant presence.

In *Juan sin tierra* the treatment of human sexuality continues where *Don Julián* left off. Yet sexuality assumes far greater importance in the last book of the trilogy through the explicit bond between writing and sexual activity. Besides referring indirectly to the writings of Paz (intertextuality), Goytisolo's reflections on this issue also demonstrate his desire to expose the inner workings of his own text. Goytisolo assimilates Paz's theories on writing and sex into his text through his constant reflections on the act of writing. At times Goytisolo seems to absorb these theories rather uncritically in an enthusiastic attempt to put theory into practice. Questions immediately arise when the reader confronts Goytisolo's enterprise: is sexuality a metaphor or a symbol for writing, or is writing actually seen as a form of sexual play? Is the energy expended during sexual activity the same as the energy devoted to the creation of a text? Perhaps one should address these questions to Said and Paz as well as to Goytisolo, for one must understand the direct source of Goytisolo's activity before one can apprehend Goytisolo himself.

For Paz, the link between language and sexuality is related to the antithesis between the body and the non-body, a conflict that is central to the understanding of Indo-European thought and behavior. Within the political, religious, economic, and ideological structures of all societies, this binomial (body/non-body) appears in some latent form. Although Paz explicitly states that the dichotomy has no meaning other than to indicate a diametric opposition, the examples that develop his notion (body versus soul, the irrational versus the rational, sexual play versus its condemnation) suggest a belief in the total freedom of the human body and in the futility of its repression, a belief also shared by Goytisolo. According to Paz, Eastern societies have found ways of integrating or fusing the dichotomy *(conjunciones),* while the West continually exaggerates the duality *(disyunciones)*. Tantric Buddhism, for example, is, in Paz's view, diametrically opposed to Christianity. While physical love is profane to Christians, Buddhists have a sacramental fascination with the erotic. The sexual differences between the masculine and the feminine in Christianity are nonexistent in Buddhism; the Buddhist, in fact, proposes to integrate the two. Nowhere is this concept seen more clearly, says Paz, than in Buddhism's treatment of bodily secretions. In the Tantric sexual ritual, for example, the man must hold back ejaculation, not for moral or hygienic reasons, but so that the semen may fuse with its opposite: emptiness.

Yet Goytisolo carries Paz's theories to conclusions that are incongruous with Paz's total project. Like the extension of Castro in *Don Julián,* Goytisolo's treatment of Paz is in no way a mechanical application. *Conjunciones y disyunciones* and *El mono gramático* undergo a basic transformation when they become intertexts within *Juan sin tierra*. Paz is concerned with the explication of certain symbols in Western and Eastern cultures for the purpose of achieving a thorough understanding of human thought and behavior. Goytisolo's project, on the other hand, is declamatory, a fact that necessarily converts Paz into a partner in Goytisolo's crime, a status that Paz may not want foisted on him.

The last volume of this treasonous trilogy is built on a series of contrasting images and concepts that re-create, in a world of fiction, what Paz discusses in his essay. Yet Goytisolo does not merely express an intellectual agreement with Paz; rather, he attempts to resolve what Paz believes are irreconcilable tensions in Western culture. Goytisolo establishes a totality of oppositions, none of which assumes central importance. The fact that the contrasts recur in different forms and become one another is evidence of Goytisolo's pronounced attempt to integrate the elements of the antagonism that he has created. Unlike Paz, who goes no further than pointing out the antagonism, Goytisolo searches for an integration.

The first chapter of *Juan sin tierra* revolves around a recurring image—the black versus the white. The self-reflective glimpses in this chapter expose the structure (p. 30): "dividirás la imaginaria escena en dos partes . . . a un lado sustantivos, adjetivos, verbos que denotan blancor, claridad, virtud : al otro, un léxico de tinieblas, negrura, pecado" ("you will divide the imaginary scene into two parts . . . on the one hand, nouns, adjectives, verbs that denote whiteness, clarity, virtue; on the other hand, a lexicon of shadows, blackness, sin," p. 20). The most glaring of these explicit structural dichotomies is the difference between the black slaves of the sugar plantation and the ruling family that looks over them. Goytisolo describes the slaves as (p. 15) "míseros rezagados procedentes del cañaveral . . . el sol del trópico cae a plomo sobre sus cabezas y se defienden de él como pueden, con pañuelos de colores y rústicos sombreros de palma . . . las hembras se abanican con femíneos gestos, coquetas siempre a pesar del polvo, la suciedad y las raídas prendas de trabajo" ("the wretched stragglers coming in from the cane fields . . . the tropical sun beats down on their heads and they shield themselves from it as best they can, with colored handkerchiefs and crudely woven hats . . . the females fan themselves with feminine gestures, eternal coquettes despite the dust, the filth, and their threadbare

work clothes," p. 6). The "limpia y virtuosa familia" (p. 15)
("pure and virtuous family," p. 6), on the other hand, is described
in the midst of a "nube de fino incienso" (p. 19) ("cloud of
delicate incense," p. 9). One of the daughters, niña Adelaida,
plays the violin, and Jorge plays the piano while another daughter
reviews her French lessons. The chaplain prays as "el criollito"
("the little mulatto boy"), another member of the family (p. 18),
"aleja incansablemente las moscas absorto en su exquisito papel de
ángel" ("tirelessly chases away the flies, totally absorbed in his
role of an exquisite cherub," p. 8). But the black–white aspect
does not take precedence over other forms of opposition. The
contrasting colors are merely a reflection of a verbal contradiction, evidenced in Paz's and Goytisolo's use of the word *sign* to
describe the binary concept: "the sign of the body and the
non-body." The contrast extends into other realms of human life
such as music and French literature. Bach, Handel, Mozart, and
Beethoven are heard in the heavens, while the queen of rhythm
dances below. In like manner, niña Fermina recites a few verses
of Lamartine to her father who does not understand French. The
poem allows the father to forget the black sinners of the
plantation (p. 34).

The chaplain, who later becomes a character named Vosk, a
further manifestation of the white or the non-body, paints a vivid
picture of the black slaves as he preaches to them. The fragments
of his sermon are interspersed throughout the chapter and add a
religious dimension to Goytisolo's antithesis. The parallel between the Cuban lords of the hacienda and divine beings is
explicit. The slave master is called "the Master on High" and his
daughter, "the White Virgin." As the sermon exposes the
mind–body, virtue–sin, and heaven–hell dichotomies, the belief
system of the ruling family and the corporeal needs of the slaves
are set off against one another. The chaplain speaks in a lofty
tone:

> no os alarméis por las penalidades que os toca sufrir : esclavo será
> vuestro cuerpo ... con el alma blanca como el blanco superior del
> azúcar : el Amo del Ingenio de Arriba os mirará con semblante

risueño y nadie os echará en cara la color prieta, el pelo pasudo, la nariz roma, los bembos bestiales . . . no maldigáis por tanto vuestra suerte ni os desconsoléis : todas esas aflicciones son necesarias al blanqueo cumplido de vuestra alma. (pp. 35, 38)

(do not be alarmed by the hardships that it is your lot to endure: your body will be enslaved . . . with a soul as white as the purest grade of sugar: the Master of the Sugar Plantation on High will look upon you with a smiling countenance, and no one will scorn you because of your dark skin, your kinky hair, your flat nose, your thick bestial lips . . . therefore do not curse your fate or lose heart: all these tribulations are necessary for the complete whitening of your souls.) (pp. 25, 27)

In the portrayal of Chaplain Vosk, the Christian faith is no less a target for Goytisolo's textual animosity in *Juan sin tierra* than in any other volume of the trilogy. Yet in the last phase of his novelistic cycle, Goytisolo's new interest in anthropology extends the subversion of Catholic Spain to a reflection on religion as a central element of the human psyche. While Vosk represents the religious aspect of the psyche, he is not the only vehicle for the expression of the author's assessment of religion. In the final division of the first chapter (pp. 51–59), Goytisolo returns to the original focus of his discourse—the photograph on the record jacket (p. 51): "la gorda cachonda del disco" ("the fat girl on the record jacket," p. 39). The author-narrator again penetrates the photo as in the first chapter division (pp. 14–15) and again inseminates the black queen. Yet the identities of all involved have changed (p. 52): the queen of rhythm has become the mother, the *tú* has become a dove, and the product of the insemination is the "bendito fruto de su vientre" ("the forever blessed fruit of her womb," p. 40). The result is a vicious parody of the Visitation of Mary. The black–white antithesis, a restatement of Paz's body/ non-body principle, has taken on a new form—a subversion of a Christian fable, on one level, and a questioning of the notion of religion, on another.

The exposition of the antithesis is far more complex in the final chapter division than in other instances, for Goytisolo draws together a variety of elements. The identities of both sides of the antithesis seem to be in a constant state of flux. The black queen changes into the blessed white virgin, and her lawful husband (Joseph) "ejerce su pobre pero decoroso oficio ... captados [Mary and Joseph] en el momento de manejar cepillo y escoplo" (p. 52) ("engages in his humble, but honest craft ... captured as the husband wields a plane and a chisel," p. 40). In like manner, the *tú* is both the inseminator (the dove) and the product of the insemination. The referent for the *tú mismo* ("you yourself") is the "bendito fruto" ("blessed fruit"). Furthermore, the *tú* (the author-narrator) has a mother ("tu futura madre") who will engender a redeemer whose name is Alvarito (p. 53). Goytisolo re-creates the biblical story within a white scenario:

> animales domésticos rematan con su benigna presencia el apacible cuadro de honradez, alegría y trabajo : su selección ha sido particularmente esmerada : un buey amable y dócil, una oveja risueña, un resucitado platero de felpa, un cordillero manso : tu futura madre canta una ingenua canción de cuna y el providencial custodio fabrica un pesebre para los propicios animales de la casa : nada más? : sí : la siempre vigilante protección del santo Angel de la Guarda planeando sobre la choza con blanquísimas alas extendidas. (p. 52)

> (domestic animals complete with their benign presence the peaceful picture of uprightness, happiness, and industrious labor: they have been selected with particular care: a gentle, docile ox, a sweet-faced ewe, a plush donkey brought back to life, a meek little lamb: your future mother is humming a simple lullaby and the provident husbandman is building a manger for the propitious animals belonging to the household: nothing more?: oh, yes, the ever-vigilant protection of the holy Guardian Angel hovering over the cabin with its snow-white wings outspread.) (p. 40)

The whiteness of the scene, however, changes to black as the reader remembers the virgin's original identity—the black queen of rhythm. The other black women spy on her and are envious of her singular privilege. They express their dislike of the chosen one in a Cuban dialect (p. 54): "qué sabrá creío la prieta étta dándoje aire de reina con esa bemba susia que tiene y su pelo pasúo y esa coló suya tan occura que no hay Dio que laclare que nosotra somo meno queya" ("who that darky think she is anyhow, puttin' on airs like a queen, with them blubber lips of hers and that kinky hair and such black skin that even the Good

Lord hisself couldn't make it no lighter," p. 42). The description of the white dove and its clean, elegant courtship of the visited one (pp. 54–55) is immediately followed by the portrayal of Changó, a deity worshiped by the slaves. Contrary to the dove, Changó is *macho* even though he wears petticoats (p. 55): "busca bronca, valiente, osado, come candela : con su bandera sangrienta, el ágil caballo moro y la flamígera espada" ("spoiling for a fight, brave, daring, breathing fire: with bloody banner, nimble Moorish steed and flaming sword," p. 43). In the description that follows, Changó kills the dove and disguises himself as the Columba in order to get at the mother who is waiting in ecstasy. The mother remains ignorant of her lover's new identity (p. 57): "Paloma mía, eres tu? : y tú : sí, mi negra, sí soy yo, tu Palomica" ("my Dove, is that you?: and you, answering: yes, it is I, your Turtledove," p. 45). Thus the black seems to overtake the white as Changó (another identity of the *tú*-author-narrator) penetrates the mother and fertilizes her. In the elaborate description that follows, all elements of black and white anxiously await the birth of the redeemer. The grotesque nativity scene, however, is anticlimactic, because the insemination of the black by the black produces the white (p. 59), a "rostro pálido aún, señorito blanco de mierda . . . ni Unigénito, ni Mesías ni Redentor" ("a paleface, a young lord and master, a motherfucking white . . . neither Unigenital nor a Messiah nor a Redeemer," p. 47). Yet the unexpected ending of the first chapter is in keeping with Goytisolo's undertaking, for it reveals not only a fusion of antithetical elements but also the primacy of the process over the product. The result of the insemination is far less grand than the act of insemination itself.

The presence of Paz's black–white or body/non-body antithesis is expressed throughout *Juan sin tierra* in a variety of forms. One of the most recurrent manifestations of the dichotomy is the contrast between cleanliness and filth, which is closely related to Goytisolo's essayistic account of the diverse ways of perceiving excrement among different cultures. In his analysis of Quevedo in *Disidencias* (pp. 117–35), Goytisolo discusses the poet's "excremental obsession" and states that the depiction of the excretion of urine, semen, and feces marks an attempt at literary humanization rather than degradation. The bodily products are the mediations between man and nature. When one confronts a monolithic ideology that turns man into an abstraction, he writes, one must remember that human beings spit, urinate, and defecate. These acts do not devalue man; on the contrary, they heighten his own consciousness of himself as a natural being. For Goytisolo, the excretory functions of the "man of flesh and bone" (suspiciously reminiscent of Unamuno) become a tool of resistance against this abstraction; they are forces of humanization (pp. 127–28). Paz's notion of the symbolic importance of excrement is similar to Goytisolo's, yet in *Juan sin tierra* excrement assumes a liberating force and becomes a tool of protest against the sexual repression of the Western world. Because bodily functions have such central importance as a synthesizing element of the body/non-body dichotomy, *Juan sin tierra* is a testimonial to the literary posture expressed in the essay.

Excrement is a product of our bodies: it belongs to us, yet it is also separate from us. This ambiguous nature of excrement is portrayed in several instances in the last volume of the trilogy. For example, a motif that appears throughout the work is a sewer. In one case Goytisolo intricately describes the labyrinthine sewer system of New York City. The antithesis that he establishes demonstrates the separation between the cleanliness above the ground and the filth below (p. 78): "en el subsuelo actual de Manhattan, a lo largo de la laberíntica red de sumideros y túneles que socava el perfil exterior de la isla, una colectividad no menos interesante y compleja . . . vive y tiende a extenderse por las densas tinieblas de su laguna Estigia" ("in the subsoil of Manhattan today, along the labyrinthine network of sewers and tunnels lying below the surface of the island, a collectivity no less interesting and complex . . . lives and attempts to propagate itself amid the dense shadows of its stygian lagoon," p. 64). The inhabitants of the city have gained true equality by the collectivity of their waste products. The sewer becomes infested with crocodiles, alligators, lizards, and iguanas, all of whom engage in procreation at random. The result of this reproduction is (p. 78) "nuevas especies anfibias, de voracidad monstruosa" ("new amphibious species, possessed of a monstrous voracity," p. 64). There is a contrast between the darkness of the sewer and the daylight above as the author-narrator expresses his desire to become one of the new species (pp. 78–79): "descolgándote por escalerillas herrumbrosas, orientándote por un dédalo de pasadizos rezumantes, asistirás a los espasmos de su cópula frí y a la ovípera eclosión de la prole : como el ojo del cíclope, tu inspiración brilla siempre de noche y el deseo de ser como ellas anida, insaciable, en lo más recóndito de tu pecho" ("letting yourself down by means of little rusty ladders, making your way through a labyrinth of slimy, oozing passages, you will witness the spasms of their cold copulation and the oviparous hatching of their offspring: like the eye of the Cyclops, your inspiration gleams brightly by night and the desire to be like them nestles, insatiable, in your most secret heart of hearts," pp. 64–65).

In one of the most outrageous scenes in which the filth–cleanliness antithesis is reenacted, Alvarito performs a miracle. After having endured an extremely painful bout of constipation, he is able to defecate an aromatic substance that smells like French perfume, not feces (p. 223). This "relic" is produced in the middle of a black–white scenario with God, the Virgin, and a multitude of angels on one side, and a serpent and King Kong on the other. Again Goytisolo reenacts a biblical scene (the temptation of Eve) as the serpent and Alvarito's guardian angel dispute the pros and cons of defecation.

SERPIENTE : por qué te obstinas en resistir a tus instintos? : no ves que te torturas en vano? : si me haces caso, experimentarás un alivio inmediato y serás inmensamente feliz

ANGEL DE LA GUARDA : el placer que te promete dura solamente unos segundos! : piensa en tu alma! : en el dolor que causarás a la Virgen! (p. 221)

(THE SERPENT: why do you stubbornly resist your instincts?: don't you

see that you are torturing yourself in vain?: if you listen to me,
you will experience immediate relief and be enormously happy

THE GUARDIAN ANGEL: the pleasure that he promises you lasts only a
few seconds!: think of your eternal soul!: of the pain that you will
cause the Virgin!) (p. 182)

The Cuban lords of the plantation are witnesses to this macabre
event and delight in the final result. The daughter, who feels that
it is her duty to speak French on such a sacred occasion, again
evokes the poetry of Lamartine:

ah, quelle volupté divine!
qué dices, hija?
que es sublime, Papá : igual igualito que un poema de
Lamartine : le haría a una creer en Dios! (p. 224)

(ah, quelle volupté divine!
what's that you say, daughter?
it's sublime, Papa: exactly like a poem by Lamartine: it's
enough to make one believe in God!) (p. 184)

The daughter has indeed "shat like a queen" (p. 10).

Goytisolo's excremental fascination is also evident in the fourth
chapter, the section of *Juan sin tierra* that most resembles *Don
Julián* in its focus on Spanish culture, especially literature. The
heading for each division is a phrase in Latin (the sacred
language) that contains a profane indictment of some aspect of
Hispanic culture. The culminating section, "Ad augusta per
angusta" (pp. 225–28), is a further exposition of the body/non-
body dichotomy, but the section also reveals Goytisolo's own
changing attitudes toward his country. This segment extends the
historical view of Spain's malaise to an anthropological analysis of
the problem. In *Juan sin tierra* Spain is viewed as a country that
has been in a perpetual state of constipation. Goytisolo reopens
the issues of *Don Julián* in an attempt to discover a solution to
Spain's ills. The *tú* now becomes a *nosotros* looking for a panacea.
No Spanish writer—"ni el melancólico self-banished Spaniard
Blanco White ni el lúcido visionario suicida [Larra]" (p. 226)
("nor our melancholy self-banished Spaniard, nor our lucid
visionary who committed suicide," p. 185)—has ever demon-

strated an awareness of the real roots of the malady. For the
tú-nosotros, however, the problem is not spiritual but biological:
the pathological inability of a country to freely remove its own
waste products—"un país secularmente estreñido" (p. 226) ("a
country constipated for centuries," p. 186). Conceived in such
terms, Spain's ills are easily cured. The *tú-nosotros* states that a
diet of raw or boiled vegetables, fruit, honey, a glass of cold water
a day, and vigorous exercise will relieve the bothersome pain. But
above all, it goes on to say:

> abandonar inmediatemente el uso del dompedro o WC . . . en lugar de
> acomodarse en un asiento horizontal a cuarenta centímetros del suelo
> . . . el sujeto (o país) extreñido debe ponerse en cuclillas . . . dicha
> postura (se lo garantizamos!) coadyuva al funcionamiento de los
> músculos abdominales . . . constituye un argumento de peso en boca
> de quienes preconizan la óptima relajación del canal y el retorno a
> los viejos, entrañables placeres de la emisión de la zanja publica" (p.
> 228)

> (ah, and above all, abandoning forthwith the use of a chamber pot or a
> flush toilet . . . instead of settling down comfortably on a horizontal
> seat some eighteen inches off the floor . . . the constipated subject (or
> country) must squat down . . . such a posture (we guarantee it!) aids
> the functioning of the abdominal muscles . . . constitutes a weighty
> argument when forthcoming from the lips of those who recommend
> the optimum relaxation of the canal and the return to the old, intimate
> pleasures of emission in common sewer ditches) (pp. 187–88)

This passage shows yet another manifestation of Goytisolo's
dichotomy: the toilet versus the open sewer.

The body/non-body antithesis illustrates the erotic nature of
writing when the body is viewed as a text. To write, for both
Goytisolo and Paz, is to affirm the body. In this analysis the
self-conscious writer who is aware of the artificiality of the task is
engaged in a form of narcissistic contemplation similar to erotic
self-stimulation. Thus writing is like sexual play in that it has no
motive, no purpose other than its own enjoyment; it is productivity without production. The idea of writing and sex as activities
with no end or goal is found not only in *Juan sin tierra* but in the
essays of *Disidencias* as well. In his study of Quevedo, Goytisolo
states that the links between the erotic impulse, excrement, and

writing can no longer be denied. He goes on to say that an unbiased study of Quevedo, a reading free of sterile and moralistic prejudice, could serve as evidence of these relationships and would in the long run free Spaniards from their traumas and ethical anguish (p. 135).

The notion of textual-sexual play is also expressed in Paz's *El mono gramático*. As the first-person narrator travels to nowhere, he experiences a wide range of sexual adventures, few of which involve heterosexual copulation among individuals of the same species. Instead, there is an array of erotic encounters of all types that have no possibility of engendering a new individual. Sexual activity is performed for no reason other than for its own sake. Again we find another form of the body/non-body dichotomy. Paz creates a scene reminiscent of Hieronymous Bosch (without the religious overtones). He divides his scenario into two panels: on top, males and females of the same species copulating; on the bottom, the copulation of a woman with males of every species except the human and with other women. "Why?" asks the narrator: repetition, analogy, exception—all these figures seem to say the same thing (pp. 73–74). Yet unlike Goytisolo's author-narrator, Paz's *yo* has no subversive intention in mind; it is content to describe a form of pantheistic unity in which all figures "seem to say the same thing." Goytisolo thus uses Paz for his own ends. The description of normal heterosexual copulation that takes place "arriba" in Paz is transformed by Goytisolo into a depiction of sterility and impotence in the portrayal of the "Reproductive Couple." These innocent newlyweds are unable to consummate their marriage because of the lack of imagination and spontaneity with which they perform the sexual act. Yet the couple holds itself in spiritual admiration and seeks the means of perpetuating its existence. They perform an uninspiring act of coitus with the sole aim of procreation as the *Manual of Healthy Sex Life* published by the Catholic Church prescribes. The sex manual is central to this scene, for it creates the direct bond between language and sex. The couple fails miserably at consummation not because they have inadequate natural instincts but because they try to do it by the book (pp. 72–73): "manual, encíclicas, gimnasia, y yoga no bastan : inútilmente ensayará nuevos ejercicios respiratorios, apurará las láminas de colores del libro, espulgará doctrinas conciliares . . . el verbo no se alzará" ("the manual, the encyclicals, gymnastics, and yoga do not suffice: in vain he will engage in further breathing exercises, scrutinize the colored illustrations in the book, read over carefully, phrase by phrase, the doctrines propounded by Church councils . . . the Word refuses to rise up," p. 59). In this scene Goytisolo ridicules the prudery and insipidness of the language of a society that seems to be incapable of sexual enjoyment.

In Goytisolo's view, writing and sexual play that are performed for a purpose are the main causes of a repressive language. The ongoing reflection on writing manifested by the Reproductive Couple is also evident in an episode in which Vosk becomes a literary critic who assesses the writing of the author-narrator. In this section literature is both form and content in Goytisolo's subversion of Vosk's system of normative aesthetics. Vosk speaks of his own literary posture:

commencé a depurar mis aficiones y gustos en el crisol de la lectura y experiencia, con lo que nació en mi pecho un amor indeleble por aquellas novelas que, combinando instrucción y deleite, son reflejo veraz y sincero de las sociedades en que se crean, merced a la introducción de personajes vivos y auténticos, sometidos a las pasiones y achaques de los hombres de carne y hueso . . . amor, digo, que me llevó al aprendizaje asiduo de los textos sagrados del realismo, en especial de las sentencias y máximas inigualables del evangelista San Lukas, gracias a las cuales mis razonamientos se robustecieron, mis dudas se disiparon, mis argumentos se articularon y mis conclusiones se fortalecieron hasta adquirir una consistencia y dureza teórica y prácticamente invulnerables. (pp. 264–65)

(I began to purify my predilections and my tastes in the crucible of reading and experience, and so it was that there was born within my breast an ineradicable love for those novels which, combining instruction with delight, are a truthful and sincere reflection of the societies in which they are created, thanks to the introduction of vivid and authentic characters, subject to the passions and the vices of men of flesh and blood . . . a love, I repeat, that led me to the diligent study of the sacred texts of realism, in particular the incomparable

apothegms and maxims of the evangelist Saint Lucaks, thanks to which
my powers of ratiocination grew stronger, my doubts evaporated, my
arguments became more reasoned, and my conclusions more firmly
supported, eventually taking on a theoretical solidity and consistency
that made them practically unassailable.) (pp. 218–19)

The parody of the theory of the "evangelist Saint Luke
(Lukács)" continues in a mock-religious tone as Vosk becomes a
confessor and makes a list of the literary sins committed by the
author-narrator: excessive use of foreign phrases; lack of linguistic
rigor; suspect representation of reality; inability to communicate
the facts coldly and objectively; meaningless accumulation of sick,
morbid personal obsessions (pp. 287–88). Vosk's literary-moral
indictment degenerates into an explicit condemnation of the
sexual behavior of the author-narrator who admits to having had
many "perverse" erotic encounters:

> con perros! con cabras! con cisnes! con dromedarios!
> cunnilingus?
> cunnilingus!
> immissio in anum?
> immissio in anum!
> coitus inter femora?
> coitus inter femora!
> fellatio?
> fellatio! (pp. 289–90)

The contrast between Vosk and the narrator is clear: Vosk's
notion of writing is prescribed and stilted; he must write for a
purpose. The narrator, on the other hand, writes and copulates
solely for pleasure.

The sexual joys of writing are made explicit throughout *Juan
sin tierra*. Goytisolo frequently interrupts a given line of discourse
to remind the reader of the intense pleasure with which he writes
his text (p. 225): "te entregas al experto onanismo de la escritura :
el inveterado, improductivo acto de empuñar la pluma y escurrir
su filiforme secreción genitiva según las pulsiones de tu
voluntad" ("you stubbornly devote yourself to the expert onanism
of writing: the inveterate, unproductive act of clutching the pen
and letting its filiform generative secretion flow in accordance

with the impulses of your will," p. 185). The comparison between writing and masturbation is a further manifestation of the purposelessness of the literary-erotic act. The ink, the generative secretion, is spilled onto the page with no goal in mind, just as the author-narrator extols the solitary pleasures of his activity (p. 298): "placer solitario de la escritura! esgrimir dulcemente la pluma, acariciarla con febrilidad adolescente . . . dejar escurrir su licor filiforme en la página en blanco . . . diferir indefinidamente el orgasmo, consumir sin mesura tu propia energía, abolir la obstinada avaricia del orden real" ("the solitary pleasure of writing! to gently wield the pen, to caress it with adolescent fervor . . . to allow its filiform liquor to trickle over the whiteness of the blank page . . . to postpone the climax indefinitely, to consume your own energy without moderation, to do away with the stubborn avarice of the real order of things," p. 249). Here the hand caresses the pen and causes the liquor to flow onto the blank page. Writing is, in this view, effortless; it is the result of an inner urge that must be relieved.[29] The hand is completely in control: it is able to prolong the orgasm and to abolish a false and unnatural order. Yet when one considers the purposes of the author-narrator's (as well as Goytisolo's) writing—to destroy what is sacred—one discovers an inherent contradiction in the project. Goytisolo advocates writing solely for pleasure, yet he constantly specifies his own destructive motives. Perhaps Goytisolo would respond to the criticism by saying that his author-narrator never writes for the *purposes* of destruction. Destruction, contamination, and subversion involve a process, a tremendously pleasurable activity, not a product.[30]

The narcissistic structure of *Juan sin tierra* reveals the changing conception of writing that develops through the trilogy. The repeated instances of self-seduction in *Don Julián*, including the ultimate unification of the contrasting characters of Alvarito and Julián, are suggestive of the self-referentiality that is brought to full fruition in *Juan sin tierra*. In *Don Julián* the seduction of Alvarito by his alter ego, Julián, is implicit; in *Juan sin tierra* erotic encounters of this nature are explicit and are integrally related to the act of writing. The most representative and intricate manifestation of self-seduction through writing is the parody of the Visitation of Mary in the first chapter. The fact that the author-narrator is a seducer as well as the result of a seduction is significant, for it unveils a theory of writing expressed throughout the text. Within the parody there is a brief interruption reminiscent of the reflections on the affinity between masturbation and writing at other points in the work. The narrator employs a linguistic person in the form of a pronoun that is found relatively infrequently—the *vosotros*. Goytisolo again lays bare the structure of his text by comparing it to an image created by a mirror:

> os habéis fijado en lo que pasa cuando os ponéis delante de un espejo? : al mismo tiempo que llegáis a él, se representa vuestra imagen dentro : y si tanto os complacéis en su vista, que os besáis a vosotros mismos en el cristal, dejaréis marcado un círculo opaco con el beso que os diereis : entonces, en un solo y único espejo se juntan tres cosas diferentes : vuestra persona, vuestra imagen y el círculo opaco formado por el beso : vosotros sois la causa de la imagen y el círculo opaco procede a la vez de vuestra persona y de la imagen producida en el espejo. (p. 53)

> (have you noticed what happens when you stand in front of a mirror?: as you approach it, your image appears in it at the same time: and if you take such delight in gazing at it that you kiss yourself on the crystal-clear surface, your kiss that you give yourselves will leave an opaque circle on it: thus, in one and the same mirror three different things are conjoined: your person, your image, and the opaque circle left by the kiss; you are the cause of the image, and the opaque circle stems both from your person and from the image produced in the mirror.) (pp. 40–41)

The three ingredients are the elements necessary for the writing of a text. The image of the writer becomes concrete with a kiss whose imprint is the embodiment of the writer's self-contemplation or self-seduction. What the reader has witnessed is the insemination of Mary, on one level, and the insemination of the text, on another. Furthermore, the results of both acts of procreation are not new entities but facsimiles of old ones. Changó reproduces a grotesque image of himself (p. 59), and the author-narrator engenders himself on the written page.

There are many conflicts in Goytisolo's linguistic enterprise. The Spanish author's search for his own identity in writing has caused the splitting of his self into a variety of entities. As Paul De Man points out, any ironic or parodic writer divides the linguistic self from the real self. *Juan sin tierra* is a testimonial to De Man's distinction, for Goytisolo has not found his true identity. He has instead confused the issue of the self by transforming himself into a multitude of selves on the written page. In the whole of the trilogy from *Señas* to *Juan sin tierra*, one detects a view of writing not only as self-reproduction but also as psychoanalytic therapy, as a tool to re-form the self into an integrated unit. The final words of the trilogy, the declaration that the author-narrator no longer has a need to write, are a testimonial to the therapeutic nature of Goytisolo's writing, as the Spanish words metamorphose into Arabic script. The last page, written wholly in Arabic, symbolizes Goytisolo's total estrangement from his pathological mother tongue. Yet in this final page there cannot be a metamorphosis from the neurotic to the sane self. Goytisolo's wish to rid himself of his hated land is doomed. His attempt at verbal suicide has failed: he will continue to write, and he will continue to do so in Spanish. The neurotic self has not been killed and will reemerge with *Makbara*.[31]

"Our Communication Has Ended"

> The composition of vast books is a laborious and impoverishing extravagance. To go on for five hundred pages developing an idea whose perfect oral exposition is possible in a few minutes! A better course of procedure is to pretend that these books already exist, and then to offer a resumé, a commentary.
>
> Jorge Luis Borges, *Ficciones*[1]

A comparison between Borges and Goytisolo uncovers an underlying difference between the two that is demonstrative of Goytisolo's literary enterprise. This quotation shows Borges's affirmation of the playful nature of writing, the happy subversion of outside texts in which the author assumes the role of an aloof and sardonic commentator of a previous style or text. Goytisolo, on the other hand, does not engage in such playfulness. His task is deadly serious. Not only does he wish to redirect what he considers to be the entire thrust of Spanish history from 711 to the present but he also searches for political, social, and religious, as well as linguistic redemption. He is deeply burdened by a culture that he once embraced but now ridicules and scorns. As he becomes increasingly aware of the impossibility of ridding himself of this culture, his hatred becomes more poignant.[2]

The bulk of Goytisolo's parodies, citations, commentaries, and transcriptions of other texts are manifestations of his attempt to corrupt and contaminate a cultural tradition. The spirit of subversion, however, is marked by a therapeutic quality incongruous with the author's purposes. The literary and biographical relationship among the protagonists of *Señas, Don Julián,* and *Juan sin tierra,* on the one hand, and Goytisolo himself, on the other, is perhaps the most telling evidence of an implicit notion of writing as psychoanalysis. *Señas* is an exposition of Alvaro's inner turmoil, a deeply psychological dilemma resulting from a series of social, political, and economic circumstances. In an attempt to relieve himself of his problems, the protagonist drinks excessively,

avoids responsibility, and wanders about his country in search of
something that he can call his own. But he never discovers that
something. In *Don Julián* the attempt to sever the link between
the protagonist and his native land takes the form of a reenactment of a historical event: the treasonous crime that opened the
doors of the mother country to an alien culture. Linguistic
treason becomes the mainstay of *Juan sin tierra* as the author-
protagonist rejoices in his newfound identity. In all three texts the
author-protagonist sees himself as a neurotic and divided individual who defames his culture in order to alleviate his personal
suffering. In the last two volumes of the trilogy he no longer
reveals his existential anguish, yet he never denies it. The
culminating pages of the final volume, the linguistic metamorphosis of Spanish into Arabic, the declaration of a definitive
change of identity, are anticlimactic. A translation of the final
words of *Juan sin tierra* reads:

> You who do not understand,
> stop following me
> our communication has ended
> I am definitively on the other side
> with the pariahs of always
> sharpening my knife[3]

From the beginning of the trilogy to the end, one of the most
frequent and significant features is the author-protagonists's state
of flux, a never-ending division, duplication, and permutation of
identities. Yet in the last section of the trilogy's final phase,
Goytisolo puts a stop to his own dynamic process of writing. He
seems unwilling to view his text as an object whose "condition is
that *it must be produced constantly*."[4] Even though intertextuality
affirms the ability of a text to change and to disguise its identity,
the end of the trilogy denies this possibility. In the final words of
Juan sin tierra, Goytisolo's world seems to freeze. The change is
permanent. There is no longer a need to write, for the exploita-
tive, oppressive, and repugnant self (an embodiment of the
Spanish language) has been killed. The verbal suicide has

accomplished what he wanted: an end to textual and existential multiplicity.

Goytisolo's bitter irony confirms Paul De Man's definition of irony as an alienating feature of literature that leads to a permanent division of the self. De Man describes this division as a reflection on insanity: "When we speak, then, of irony originating at the cost of the empirical self, the statement has to be taken seriously enough to be carried to the extreme: absolute irony is a consciousness of madness, itself the end of all consciousness; it is a consciousness of a non-consciousness, a reflection of madness from the inside of madness itself."[5] Goytisolo's intertextual irony, the textual masks that he wears in order to conceal his subversion of a tradition, intensifies this state of madness. His self is divided not into two but into many, a fact that further complicates the deranged nature of his writing.

The "reflection on madness from the inside of madness" cannot take on a therapeutic value. Yet toward the end of the trilogy, Goytisolo shows his unwillingness to accept this maxim. His glorious self-annihilation is intended as an attempt at reconciliation of the plurality of selves. The final act is a mediation between the destruction of sacred Spain inside the act of writing and outside it. In the culminating pages, art is reconciled with the world. The exiled Spanish author longs for this recovery throughout his linguistic journey and truly believes that the search has ended joyously. Goytisolo's sense of his own self-integration, his oneness with the world, unravels, however, when we take into consideration an important consequence of ironic discourse: the awareness of inauthenticity does not presuppose authenticity.[6] Although Goytisolo mimics his predecessors and subverts their intentions; although he praises the literary figures whom he abhors; although he infiltrates a previous text, corrupts its meaning, and disguises himself as an embodiment of the very culture he violates; all these techniques cannot permanently relieve the anguish and alienation that inspired the series of assaults. The perverse pleasure that he receives from these acts of treason is momentary and ultimately heightens the tension that caused them. The eventual result can only be further rebellion and aggression—a perpetual regeneration of linguistic subversion.

A few years after the completion of *Juan sin tierra*, Goytisolo remarked that the "ganas de escribir" ("urge to write") had not affected him since the completion of the trilogy.[7] He believed himself cured of a malady that had plagued him throughout his life. Feeling at one with himself, he spent his time traveling to the corners of the Arabian world that continued to fascinate him.[8] Although he wrote a few essays (*Disidencias*) in which he re-created in coherent and logical prose the themes and concerns of his fiction, he produced nothing that approached the style and scope of *Juan sin tierra*. But this state of self-gratification was short-lived, for Goytisolo had not resolved his problem, he had only created new ones. The texts that he believed he had destroyed, including his own, were not dead. After a brief period of rest, Goytisolo became aware of the contradiction. In the prologue to a new book of political essays, *Libertad, libertad, libertad* (1978), he states:

> In spite of all my efforts to remain in the margins of the problem of Spain, it was impossible to do so. Spain came back to haunt me in my most grave moments with its destructive force. I am referring to the resurgence of my indignation against all that official Spain represented, the same indignation of old, as if the only possible link between myself and my country were, after all these years, that oppressive feeling of frustration, impotence, and rage of which I ingenuously thought myself cured and which, after having poisoned me since adolescence, threatened to escort me to my grave. Being Spanish has always been for me, and probably for many others, a fate both sad and grotesque, an endemic disease that, after a period of insidiously deceptive tranquility, reemerged, at times with irrepressible violence. (p. 8)

In these words lie the seeds of a new linguistic derangement. In the new neurosis, in the new textual mask of *Makbara*, in the new Goytisolo are the remnants of the old. Juan sin Tierra still writes.

Notes

Notes to the Introduction

1. Further references to *Señas de identidad, Reivindicación del Conde don Julián,* and *Juan sin tierra* are in the text. See "A Note on the Translations" on p. vi. The concept of intertextuality and Goytisolo's theoretical and practical understanding of it are discussed in Chapter 1.

2. *Juegos* has been published in English as *The Young Assassins,* trans. John Rust (New York: Knopf, 1959). Further references to *Juegos de manos* and *Duelo en el paraíso* are in the text.

3. According to José María Castellet, "Veinte años de novela española," *Cuadernos Americanos* 126 (1963): 290–95, post-civil-war novelists may be divided into two groups: those who were old enough to have experienced the war firsthand (Cela, Laforet, Matute), and those who were so young that their re-creation of the war is a haunting childhood memory (Rafael Sánchez Ferlosio, Luis and Juan Goytisolo, Juan Marsé). This dichotomy is deceptive because it is based solely on biographical and thematic data. If one considers stylistic factors, it is clear that all Spanish writers who published in the forties and fifties show an intense preoccupation with reality in an attempt to distance themselves from the fantasy and verbal artifice of the previous generation.

4. *Problemas de la novela,* p. 86. This book, a collection of essays that had been published in the weekly journal *Destino* between 1956 and 1959, is not nearly as severe as Aub's attack on Ortega in *Discurso de la novela española contemporánea,* pp. 81–99. Yet the thrust of Goytisolo's arguments as well as his personal admiration for Aub indicate that the two criticisms of Ortega are closely related. See Ortega's *La deshumanización del arte* (Madrid: Revista de Occidente, 1925).

5. In this early period, Goytisolo was influenced by Alain Robbe-Grillet's *For a New Novel.* Ramón Buckley in *Problemas formales de la novela española contemporánea* (p. 41) states that Robbe-Grillet's new "objectivist" novel "nos ofrece un mundo de objetos, pero no nos ofrece una interpretación . . . se ocupa de una realidad sin mito" ("offers us a world of objects, but does not give us an interpretation . . . it deals with a reality without myth"). He also points out how Goytisolo embraces certain tenets of Robbe-Grillet's theory. The ultimate manifestation of objectivism in Spain is Rafael Sánchez Ferlosio's *El Jarama* (Barcelona: Destino, 1956). While the narratives of Goytisolo's early novels are never as objective and as seemingly mundane as that of *El Jarama,* Sánchez Ferlosio did exert an influence on the young Goytisolo.

6. Introduction to *Fiestas*, p. 9. Further references to this book are in the text.

7. Further references to *El circo* and *La resaca* are in the text.

8. The complete Spanish text of Machado's poem is taken from *Poesías completas* (Madrid: Espasa-Calpe, 1969), pp. 152–53. My translation was done with the aid of Margaret Sayers Peden. Machado also wrote a poem called "El pasado efímero," but its presence in Goytisolo is not felt as strongly as that of "El mañana efímero."

9. Professor Ortega may be remotely related to Ortega y Gasset in his liberal outlook on Spanish politics, yet, unlike the philosopher, he is an activist. He is a man who attempts to synthesize theory and practice, a synthesis that is central to the social philosophy of Giner de los Ríos.

10. Fernando de los Ríos, ed., *El pensamiento de Giner de los Ríos*. See especially "Problemas urgentes de nuestra educación nacional" (pp. 126–52) and "El espíritu de la institución libre" (pp. 105–7).

11. It is significant that a utopian notion of social peace is an important aspect of Giner de los Ríos's thought. See Juan López-Morillas, ed., *Giner de los Ríos: Ensayos*.

12. Further references to *Campos de Níjar, La isla, La Chanca*, and *Pueblo en marcha* are in the text.

13. Kessel Schwartz, "Stylistic and Psychosexual Constants in the Novels of Juan Goytisolo," p. 119. "*Juan sin tierra*: Esperpento anal," in Julián Ríos, ed., *Juan sin tierra*, p. 83.

14. The first edition of *Señas* contains a chapter that takes place in Cuba. Goytisolo decided to omit this chapter from the second edition (1969). For a penetrating study of the differences between the two editions and of Goytisolo's reasons for revising his work, see Maryellen Bieder, "A Case of Altered Identity: Two Editions of Juan Goytisolo's *Señas de identidad*," *Modern Language Notes* 89 (1974): 298–310.

15. The personal changes in Goytisolo as well as the changes in his writing are revealed in an interview with Emir Rodríguez Monegal, "Destrucción de la España sagrada," pp. 46–60. This interview is an important topic in my discussion of *Señas* in Chapter 2.

16. For the most thorough analysis of the destructive-creative process in Goytisolo, see Linda Levine, *Juan Goytisolo: La destrucción creadora*. Even though Levine does not deal with *Juan sin tierra*, her book is the best study of Goytisolo's later writing to date and has accomplished much of the groundwork for other critical essays, including my own.

Notes to Chapter 1

1. Julián Ríos, ed., *Juan Goytisolo*, p. 15.

2. Interview with Emir Rodríguez Monegal, "Destrucción de la España sagrada," p. 50.

3. Further references to *Problemas de la novela* are in the text.

Parenthetical text references to *El furgón de cola* are to the Paris edition. Further references to *Disidencias* are in the text.

4. See Susan Sontag's preface to Roland Barthes, *Writing Degree Zero*, pp. xiv–xx.

5. For a concise overview of nineteenth-century views of literary history, see Claudio Guillén, "The Aesthetics of Literary Influence," in *Literature as System*, pp. 17–27. See also René Wellek and Austin Warren, *Theory of Literature*, pp. 38–45, 252–69. Harold Bloom's *The Anxiety of Influence: A Theory of Poetry* deals with literary relationships and situates the concept of influence within the context of Freudian psychoanalysis and Nietzschean philosophy.

6. Quoted in an essay by Eichenbaum, "Theory of the Formal Method," in Ladislav Matejka and Krystyna Pomorska, eds. and trans., *Readings in Russian Poetics: Formalist and Structuralist Views*, p. 31. Further references to the Russian formalist essays in this collection are in the text.

7. For a detailed explanation of the polemic, see Victor Erlich, *Russian Formalism*.

8. Jonathan Culler, *Structuralist Poetics: Structuralism, Linguistics and the Study of Literature*, p. 27.

9. Ibid., p. 29. For a clear exposition of the notion of authorship and the structuralists' rejection of the self, see Eugenio Donato, "Structuralism: The Aftermath," pp. 9–26.

10. Julia Kristeva, *Le texte du roman: Approche sémiologique d'une structure discursive transformationnelle*, p. 12. Although this book was published in 1970, it was written before those other works for which Kristeva is more widely known: *Semiotikè: Recherches pour une sémanalyse* (Paris: Seuil, 1969) and *La révolution du langage poétique; l'avant-garde à la fin du XIXe siècle: Lautréamont et Mallarmé* (Paris: Seuil, 1974). *Le texte du roman* sets the framework for further elaboration to which this notion of textuality is central. Subsequent references to this book are in the text. Kristeva employs the term *langue* in the structuralist sense, to distinguish it from *langage*. The latter refers to the entire gamut of communication, while the former denotes a specific language system.

11. See Ferdinande de Saussure, "Course in General Linguistics," in Richard T. De George and Fernande M. De George, eds., *The Structuralists: From Marx to Lévi-Strauss*, pp. 59–79.

12. Poststructuralism, an offshoot or the "aftermath" of structuralism, emphasizes this characteristic of the sign and questions the feasibility of codifying all literature and rendering its study scientific. (See Culler, *Structuralist Poetics*, pp. 241–54.) Structuralists and poststructuralists, however, share a basic concern for semiotics as the point of departure for any literary study.

13. Tzvetan Todorov, "Introduction," pp. 1–4. Todorov introduces various articles on *vraisemblance,* including one by Kristeva ("La

productivité dite texte," pp. 58–83), by defining the term. Further references to this issue are in the text.

14. Roland Barthes, *S/Z*, p. 80.
15. In *Théorie d'ensemble*, pp. 297–316. Further references to this essay are in the text.
16. Barthes, *S/Z*, p. 10.
17. Ibid., p. 11.
18. Roland Barthes, *The Pleasure of the Text*, pp. 35–36.
19. Edward W. Said, *Beginnings: Intention and Method*, p. 218.
20. Roland Barthes, *Critical Essays*, p. 97. Barthes's distinction between old and new literature is arbitrary. A glimpse at *Don Quijote*'s "Scrutiny of the Books" is ample evidence. Important here is the difference between self-conscious and non-self-conscious literature.
21. Further references to the article are in the text.
22. Barthes, *Critical Essays*, p. 97.
23. See Severo Sarduy, *Escrito sobre un cuerpo* and "El barroco y el neo-barroco," pp. 178–81. Further references to these essays are in the text.

Notes to Chapter 2

1. Goytisolo has said in interviews that he shares certain ideas about literature with the modern French critics (Barthes, Gérard Gennette, Todorov, Phillipe Sollers, and the *Tel Quel* group); specifically, he has indicated that they influenced his new mode of writing that began with *Señas*. He objects, however, to people who write novels according to a theoretical prescription. See Julio Ortega, "An Interview with Juan Goytisolo," p. 77; also in *Disidencias*, pp. 289–325. In addition, see José Hernández, "Juan Goytisolo," p. 339. The direct effect of the structuralists on Goytisolo cannot be denied. There are many points in his essays that testify to his espousal of certain poststructuralist ideas: the notion of writing as an erotic act, a motif that permeates *Disidencias* ("Notas sobre *La lozana andaluza*," "El lenguaje del cuerpo," "La metáfora erótica"); and the argument that writing and certain usages of language can be acts of revolution (*El furgón*, pp. 51, 56; *Disidencias*, pp. 34, 246–61). Also pertinent is the frequency with which Goytisolo makes flattering reference in *Disidencias* to the Russian formalists and to Barthes, Sollers, Gilles Deleuze, Emile Benveniste, and other members of the Parisian structuralist club. See *Disidencias*, notes 2, 4, 18 (p. 35); 6 (p. 61); 8, 10, 12, 13, 14, 20, 23, 36 (pp. 109–15); 1, 2, 3, 9, 10 (p. 169); 9 (p. 192); 3 (p. 219); 4, 9, 10 (pp. 284–85); and in *El furgón* (pp. 117–39), see "Lenguaje, realidad ideal y realidad efectiva," which demonstrates a rather poor assimilation of Saussurian linguistics. See also Genaro Pérez's *Formalist Elements in the Novels of Juan Goytisolo*.
2. In a personal interview with Goytisolo during July 1977, I asked him to explain the relationship between his writing and that of

contemporary Latin American writers such as Sarduy, Paz, and Fuentes. His response was that his writing bore greater resemblance to the work of the Latin Americans than to that of the Spaniards insofar as he was actively engaged in a "search for language."
3. Julián Ríos, ed., *Juan Goytisolo*, p. 142.
4. "Declaración de Juan Goytisolo," *Norte* 13, nos. 4–6 (1972): 94.
5. For the most part, this essay is one of Goytisolo's worst. Not only are the theoretical concepts unclear but also there has been no attempt to synthesize the discussion of *Don Quijote* with that of *TTT*. The analysis would have been better presented as two separate essays.
6. Juan Goytisolo, "Presentación crítica de la obra de José María Blanco White," pp. 1–98. Further references are in the text.
7. In his political as well as social articles, Larra constantly compares Spain to Europe in the process of building political democracy. See "En este país," "La calamidad europea," "Nadie pase sin hablar al portero," and a series of articles, "De un liberal de acá a un liberal de allá," in *Artículos completos*.
8. Ibid., p. 1264.
9. Ibid., p. 1162. In the last paragraph of Larra's article, there is a satiric proliferation of the word *entusiasmo*, used in a variety of contexts (p. 1165). See Goytisolo's use of the word in *El furgón* (p. 23): "el silencio nos llena de entusiasmo" ("the silence fills us with enthusiasm").
10. Jorge Luis Borges, *Ficciones*, p. 44.

Notes to Chapter 3

1. Interview with Emir Rodríguez Monegal, "Destrucción de la España sagrada," pp. 46–60. Further references to this interview are in the text.
2. See Chap. 1, pp. 34–35.
3. See my comments on Schwartz in the Introduction.
4. Further references to Emile Benveniste, *Problems in General Linguistics,* are in the text. In the interview with José Hernández, "Juan Goytisolo," p. 339, Goytisolo expressed his interest in Benvenistian linguistics. See also Julián Ríos, ed., *Juan Goytisolo*, p. 127.
5. In Richard T. De George and Fernande M. De George, eds., *The Structuralists: From Marx to Lévi-Strauss,* pp. 154–67.
6. Ibid., p. 161.
7. As I use these terms, the *main text* is the work under discussion, the work that contains the other texts. The *outside text* is the cited or previous text that exists outside of the main text. The *intertext* refers to that aspect of the outside text that appears within the main text.
8. The readings of Spengler, Keyserling, Baudelaire, and Verlaine are, of course, misreadings. For some readers, Spengler is a radical, and Baudelaire a reactionary. Again Goytisolo's personal misreading evidences a certain blindness and superficiality in the interpretation of the outside text in an attempt to advance his own position.

9. Goytisolo donated much of the material that he employed in the writing of his novels to the Special Collection of the Murgar Library at Boston University. Among these pamphlets, newspaper clippings, photographs, and letters is a collection of stories of martyred saints from which this passage is taken. Further references to these sources are cited in the text as "SCML." The bibliography in Linda Levine's *Juan Goytisolo: La destrucción creadora* organizes this material (pp. 300–301), as does Francisco Carenas's bibliography in Ríos, ed., *Juan Goytisolo*, pp. 207–66.

10. The original letter was written to Goytisolo's great-grandfather and may be found in the SCML. While the handwriting is not easily deciphered, its impact on Goytisolo, the young rebel writer, is apparent: "Mi amor, su merse . . . me dejó en casa de sus hijos Ferminita y el niño Agustín y yo hice todos los posibles [*sic*] de cumplir con la palabra que yo di a su merse pero cuando vino la niña Telesfina en casa de la niña Ferminita me botaron [*sic*] de la casa y aquí estoy como quiera en la calle esperando a su merse . . . su esclaba [*sic*], Casilda Goytisolo" ("My love, my master . . . you left me in the house of your children Ferminita and little Agustín and I did all that I could to keep my master's word but when little Telesfina came to Ferminita's house they threw me out of the house and here I am in the street waiting for my master . . . Your slave, Casilda Goytisolo"). In a note in the margin, Juan Goytisolo wrote that Agustín Goytisolo (his grandfather) was a rich sugar-plantation owner who left a great fortune to his numerous offspring. References to this letter are found in the subsequent volumes of the trilogy; see especially pp. 313–14 of *Juan sin tierra*.

11. The complete diary is found in the SCML.

12. There are numerous newspaper clippings concerning this polemic in the SCML. L. Levine also points out the importance of these newspaper items in *Juan Goytisolo: La destrucción creadora*, pp. 124–26.

13. See Chap. 1, pp. 29–39.

14. These words appear in the form of an epigraph to *Señas*. They are taken from Luis Cernuda's poem "Limbo" (see Chap. 1). It is interesting that in the Rodríguez Monegal interview Goytisolo says that he had originally intended to title the first volume of the trilogy "Mejor la destrucción, el fuego."

Notes to Chapter 4

1. Emir Rodríguez Monegal, "Destrucción de la España sagrada."

2. In the Special Collection, Murgar Library, Boston University (SCML), there are numerous letters from Castro to Goytisolo and vice versa. In this correspondence we are made aware of a personal and affectionate relationship between the novelist and the historian. See also Goytisolo's essay, "Supervivencias tribales en el medio intelectual español," in *Estudios sobre la obra de Américo Castro,* pp. 143–56; also see *Disidencias*, pp. 137–49. See my analysis of the Goytisolo–Castro

connection, "Juan Goytisolo: Unruly Disciple of Américo Castro," pp. 353–64.

3. See Goytisolo's introduction to *Blanco White* (pp. 1–98) and the essays on Larra (pp. 7–20) and Cernuda (pp. 99–116) in *El furgón*.

4. This book marks a break in Castro's thinking. Until 1939 he had been primarily concerned with the relationship between Spain and the European Renaissance. *España en su historia* is the result of a reassessment of the problem of Spain, a new perspective that reaches its culmination in *La realidad histórica de España*. Further references to *La realidad* are in the text.

5. Later I speak in detail about Seneca's presence in *Don Julián*.

6. "La España de Fernando de Rojas" in *Disidencias*, pp. 13–35. The critical controversy over *La Celestina* still rages. See Ciriaco Morón-Arroyo's *Sentido y forma de* La Celestina (Madrid: Cátedra, 1974), pp. 17–35, in which the author reviews the disparate interpretations *La Celestina* has elicited (existentialist, moralistic, formal, generic). Further references are in the text.

7. Stephen Gilman, *The Spain of Fernando de Rojas*.

8. In *Juan Goytisolo: La destrucción creadora*, Linda Levine discusses the strong affinity between Castro and Goytisolo and comments specifically on the textual similarities between *La realidad* and *Don Julián*, but her analysis does not delve deeply into this relationship.

9. (Madrid: Revista de Occidente, 1968).

10. Vol. 1, pp. 307–10.

11. Immediately apparent in this quotation is Goytisolo's new writing style, especially the use of colons in lieu of periods. The omission of the period evidences a radical departure from the rules of writing, a preference for fragments over sentences. In this passage, as in the whole of *Don Julián*, the objects described affirm their own artificiality.

12. Fray Luis de León's poem "Oda a Salinas" is an example of a sixteenth-century text in which the poet evokes music as an attempt to reach the heavens.

13. There is an attempt in Ortega y Gasset to elevate the custom of bullfighting to the realm of philosophy (p. 135): "El valor en el gran torero no tiene nada que ver con la inconsciencia de cualquier mozo insensato, sino que en todo instante se halla bien fundado, como diría Leibniz, a saber, fundado en la lúcida percepción de lo que el toro está queriendo decir" ("The valor of a great bullfighter has nothing to do with the insensibility of a foolish youngster, but the fact that at all times he is well grounded, as Leibniz would say, in the lucid understanding of what the bull is trying to say"). In *Juan Goytisolo: La destrucción creadora* (pp. 161–62), L. Levine points out the presence of this text within *Don Julián*.

14. Angel Ganivet, *Idearium español*, pp. 10, 58.

15. See p. 34 in *Don Julián*. These words are an allusion to the Generation of '98, especially Unamuno in his search for the eternal Spanish essence.

16. Gonzalo Sobejano, "*Don Julián*, iconoclasta de la literatura patria," pp. 7–14. Sobejano divides the intertexts of *Don Julián* into "positive," "negative," and "neutral" categories, but he provides no in-depth explanation for these divisions and accepts them far too readily.

17. Larra wrote in *Artículos completos* (pp. 1271–72) that these human qualities can be attributed to the "desgracia del país mismo" ("the misfortune of the country itself").

18. José Ortega, *Alienación y agresión en "Señas de identidad" y "Reivindicación del Conde don Julián*," p. 139. In *Juan Goytisolo: La destrucción creadora*, L. Levine correctly pinpoints many instances of parody, but no theoretical explanation is given.

19. See Chap. 2, note 1.

20. See especially pp. 158–60. Further references are in the text.

21. *Casticismo* refers to a highbred Castilian essence and is a derivative of the word "caste" as well as of *castizo*, meaning "pure Castilian."

22. *Obras completas*, 1: 775. Further references to *Casticismo* in the text are from the edition published by Escelicer in 1966.

23. For the works of Azorín, see *Obras selectas*, pp. 279–345, 561–607. In *Una hora de España*, the reader finds (p. 575): "El genio de España no podrá ser comprendido sin la consideración de este ir y venir de los rebaños por montañas y llanuras. . . . Agrada encontrar y manejar los vocablos con que se denominan los accidentes y particularidades del campo y de la montaña. Gustamos sabor de España en esos vocablos" ("Spain's genius cannot be understood without considering the comings and goings of these flocks [of sheep] over the mountains and plains. . . . It's pleasing to find and use the words that designate the accidents and particularities of fields and mountains. We may savor the taste of Spain in these words"). Although Goytisolo's sympathy for Machado is expressed in the early works, the poet of the Generation of '98 is not a positive figure in *Don Julián*. He is rather seen as one who is unable to rid himself of the idea of the Castilian essence. It is interesting that Goytisolo did not include Ramón del Valle-Inclán in his harsh assessment of the Generation of '98. For Goytisolo, Valle stands in contrast to Unamuno, Azorín, and Machado. His presence in *Don Julián* is felt in Goytisolo's evocation of the grotesque (pp. 145–48). See Goytisolo's article, "La audacia estética de Valle-Inclán," in the SCML.

24. These words are taken from a newspaper clipping in the SCML titled "Madrid ha hecho penitencia al estilo de la Edad Media" ("Madrid Has Done Penance in the Style of the Middle Ages").

25. Also implicit here is the blend of the old and the new. The concept of dialogue in the Renaissance (Juan de Valdés, for example) was very close to doctrine. Goytisolo throws the unification of these two concepts (dialogue and doctrine) out of balance by placing them in a twentieth-century context.

26. Miguel de Cervantes, *Don Quijote de la Mancha*, ed. Martín de Riquer, pp. 66–77. Goytisolo's statement appeared in an interview with José Hernández, "Juan Goytisolo," pp. 342–43.

27. Compare with Cervantes, *Don Quijote*, pp. 870–73.
28. The ending of the final volume of the trilogy, *Juan sin tierra*, also engages in this kind of linguistic deformation.

Notes to Chapter 5

1. Robert Alter, *Partial Magic: The Novel as a Self-conscious Genre*, p. x.
2. Paul De Man, "The Rhetoric of Temporality," pp. 173–209.
3. Ibid., p. 196.
4. To my knowledge, David Herzberger is the only critic of Goytisolo's writing who discusses this contradiction. See "The Theoretical Disparity of Contemporary Spanish Narrative," pp. 215–29, especially pp. 218–20. In my appraisal of Goytisolo, I am probably closer to Herzberger than to any other critic.
5. As *Don Julián* progresses, it becomes clear that these forces will ultimately lead to self-destruction. Robert Spires's analysis of the self-destructive elements of the novel adds an important dimension to Linda Levine's discussion of creative destruction in *Juan Goytisolo: La destrucción creadora*. See Spires, "La autodestrucción creativa en *Reivindicación del Conde don Julián*," pp. 191–202. See also his *La novela española de posguerra: Creación artística y experiencia social*, pp. 281–304.
6. Lane's translation is loose; the Spanish literally means "the word freed of secular servitude."
7. Spires, *La novela española*, pp. 285, 287–88. Spires also speaks of a *desdoblamiento* of the protagonist but does not discuss how this doubling affects the relationship among author, narrator, and protagonist, nor does he situate this split in the context of the act of writing—the real self versus the written self.
8. In an attempt to come to grips with new developments in modern literature, Richard Poirier in *The Performing Self: Compositions and Decompositions in the Languages of Contemporary Life*, pp. 27–28, writes: "As against these recognized forms of parody, I want to define a newly developed one—a literature of self-parody that makes fun of itself as it goes along. . . . While parody has traditionally been anxious to suggest that life or history or reality has made certain styles outmoded, the literature of self-parody, quite unsure of the relevance of such standards, makes fun of the effort to verify them by the act of writing."
9. In an interview with Julio Ortega in Julián Ríos, ed., *Juan Goytisolo*, pp. 121–36, Goytisolo stated (p. 128) that *Juan sin tierra* was the "finis terrae de mi propia escritura" ("the end of my own writing"). He makes this point again in a more recent interview with Julián Ríos, "Desde *Juan sin tierra*," in Julián Ríos, ed., *Juan sin tierra*, pp. 9–10.
10. See Chap. 3, note 10.
11. After the publication of *Juan sin tierra*, many articles deluged the field of twentieth-century peninsular studies. Some of these appeared in

Ríos, ed., *Juan sin tierra*, but the one that stands out for its profundity and lucidity, in my opinion, is not in that collection: Robert Spires, "Latrines, Whirlpools, and Voids: The Metafictional Mode of *Juan sin tierra*," pp. 151–69. Spires's understanding of the term *metafiction* embodies essentially the same concept as do the words I use—self-reflection, self-consciousness, and self-referentiality. There are points, however, on which Spires and I disagree. For example, he never seems to question Goytisolo's total novelistic enterprise. He rather ingenuously submits that "*Juan sin Tierra* . . . is a novel about itself, a metafiction challenging *and ultimately negating* the communicative capacity of language" (p. 151, emphasis added). I would ask Spires this question: Does Goytisolo really believe that by writing a novel, a communicative act, he is denying the existence of communication? In spite of Derrida, we do speak, write, read, and listen, and when we do, we assume (or at least hope) that part of what we transmit or receive will be understood. Does not Goytisolo operate under the same assumption even when he writes in Arabic?

12. Ríos, ed., *Juan Goytisolo*, pp. 126–27.
13. "La desterritorialización" in ibid., pp. 180–81.
14. This *tú*, the protagonist-narrator and author, is one of the important elements of the work. In this study I employ the words *tú* and "author-narrator" when I refer to this central literary element.
15. Ríos, ed., *Juan Goytisolo*, p. 125.
16. Francis B. Carmody, ed., *Jean sans terre*, p. 6. It is interesting that the translator was none other than Manuel Altolaguirre, another Spanish-civil-war exile.
17. We are reminded of the presence of Góngora and Larra in *Don Julián* as allies of the author. While these textual alliances are exceptions in *Don Julián*, they are dominant in *Juan sin tierra*.
18. Lawrence's love for Arab culture was more than a fascination for the exotic. Like Goytisolo, he considered the Arab mode of existence a part of his inner being: "I was sent to these Arabs as a stranger, unable to think their thoughts or subscribe their beliefs, but charged by duty to lead them forward and to develop to the highest any movement of theirs profitable to England in her war. If I could not assume their character, I could at least conceal my own, and pass among them without evident friction, neither a discord nor a critic but an unnoticed influence. Since I was their fellow, I will not be their apologist or advocate. Today in my old garments, I could play the bystander, obedient to the sensibilities of our theatre . . . but it is more honest to record that these ideas and actions then passed naturally" (pp. 28–29).
19. Ríos, ed., *Juan Goytisolo*, p. 125.
20. Since the original Catalan text is lost, the most authentic version of the *Disputa* is a French translation first published by R. Foulché-Delbosc, "Disputation de l'asne," *Revue Hispanique* 24 (1911): 358–479.

21. Ibid., pp. 385–86.
22. The translation reads: "Your Lords would be maggots because they eat you, as would . . . all the other animals and birds and fish of the sea, because they eat you, and your Lords would be Wolves, Dogs, and many other animals. And what is even worse, lice, bedbugs, and nits would be your Lords, because they all eat your flesh" (p. 411).
23. *Lettres à Mme de Bondy.*
24. His letters are written as prayers (p. 155): "Cette Afrique, . . . ces millions d'infidèles, . . . appellent tellement la sainteté qui seule obtiendra leur conversion; priez pour que je me convertisse et me sanctifie, ainsi que les autres prêtres si peu nombreux hélas qui s'occupent d'eux, afin que la bonne Nouvelle arrive enfin et que ces derniers venus se présentent enfin à la crèche de Jésus pour adorer à leur tour" ("this Africa . . . these millions of infidels, call forth so irresistibly the saintliness that will be the means of converting them; pray that I may be converted and sanctified, as well as the other priests, so few in number, alas, who care about them; that the Good News be heard and that these latecomers arrive in their turn at Christ's manger in adoration"). Goytisolo mimicks this religious tone by incorporating certain phrases from the original texts of the letters. The fact that Foucauld's writing appears in the original French is reminiscent of the textual "encrustations" and interpolations that were present in *Señas.*
25. Further references to *Conjunciones y disyunciones* and to *El mono gramático* are in the text. An article by Susan F. Levine, " 'Cuerpo' y 'no cuerpo'—Una conjunción entre Juan Goytisolo y Octavio Paz," pp. 123–35, offers a lucid exposition of the themes in *Juan sin tierra* that emanate from Paz's *Conjunciones,* although she does not consider *Mono.* While she concludes that Goytisolo's views and Paz's "coincide" (pp. 132, 134), I believe, as we shall see, that Goytisolo's intentions are distinct from Paz's. The two views are certainly not mutually exclusive, but they are different nonetheless. See also Jerome Bernstein, "Cuerpo, lenguaje y divinidad," in Ríos, ed., *Juan sin tierra,* pp. 151–69.
26. See also Goytisolo's "Sobre 'Conjunciones y Disyunciones,' " pp. 169–75.
27. Much of the material concerning self-reflection in *Don Julián* and *Juan sin tierra* is taken from my article, "Juan Goytisolo's Mirrors: Intertextuality and Self-reflection in *Reivindicación del Conde don Julián* and *Juan sin tierra.*"
28. Edward W. Said, *Beginnings: Intention and Method,* p. 263.
29. Goytisolo refers to this inner urge as "ganas de escribir" in his interview with Julián Ríos in Ríos, ed., *Juan sin tierra,* p. 11.
30. Spires also discusses the problem of "process" and "product" in *Juan sin tierra*; see "Latrines, Whirlpools, and Voids."
31. Goytisolo's first novel of the eighties proves my point. At first reading, *Makbara* is reminiscent of the Goytisolo who wrote *Señas, Don Julián,* and *Juan sin tierra.*

Notes to "Our Communication Has Ended"

1. Jorge Luis Borges, *Ficciones,* p. 15.
2. The differences between Borges and Goytisolo illustrate the distance between the Spanish author and his Latin American counterparts (Manuel Puig, Julio Cortázar, Guillermo Cabrera Infante). Although Goytisolo continues to declare his affinity with these writers and while his conception of writing as a subversive activity is akin to that of certain Latin Americans, Goytisolo's cultural roots are far more important to him. For this reason, his task is far more somber: behind the aloofness and playfulness is always his cultural and existential turmoil.
3. The Spanish translation is found in Linda Levine, *"Juan sin tierra:* Goytisolo se retrata,"* in Julián Ríos, ed., *Juan sin tierra,* p. 47.
4. Edward W. Said, *Beginnings: Intention and Method,* p. 197.
5. Paul De Man, "The Rhetoric of Temporality," p. 198.
6. Ibid., p. 203.
7. Ríos, ed., *Juan sin tierra,* p. 11.
8. Personal conversation with Goytisolo, July 1977.

Bibliography

Fiction and Essays by Juan Goytisolo (in chronological order)

Juegos de manos. Barcelona: Destino, 1954.
Duelo en el paraíso. Barcelona: Planeta, 1955.
El circo. Barcelona: Destino, 1957.
Problemas de la novela. Barcelona: Seix Barral, 1959.
Campos de Níjar. Barcelona: Seix Barral, 1960.
La isla. Barcelona: Seix Barral, 1961.
La resaca. Mexico: Mortiz, 1961.
Fin de fiesta. Barcelona: Seix Barral, 1962.
La Chanca. Paris: Librería Española, 1962.
Pueblo en marcha. Paris: Librería Española, 1963.
Fiestas. New York: Dell, 1964.
Señas de identidad. Mexico: Mortiz, 1966, 1969.
El furgón de cola. Paris: Ruedo Ibérico, 1967; Barcelona: Seix Barral, 1976.
Reivindicación del Conde don Julián. Mexico: Mortiz, 1970.
"Supervivencias tribales en el medio intelectual español." In *Estudios sobre la obra de Américo Castro.* Edited by Pedro Laín Entralgo, pp. 141–56. Madrid: Taurus, 1970.
"Presentación crítica de la obra de José María Blanco White." In *Blanco White, obra inglesa,* pp. 1–98. Barcelona: Seix Barral, 1972.
"Declaración de la mesa redonda celebrada en la Universidad de Wisconsin–Parkside." *Norte* 13, nos. 4–6 (1972): 91–96.
"Sobre 'Conjunciones y Disyunciones.' " *Revista Iberoamericana* 41 (April–June 1975): 169–75.
Juan sin tierra. Barcelona: Seix Barral, 1975.
Disidencias. Barcelona: Seix Barral, 1977.
Personal interview. July 1977.
Libertad, libertad, libertad. Barcelona: Anagrama, 1978.
Makbara. Barcelona: Seix Barral, 1980.
Juan Goytisolo Archives. Special Collection, Murgar Library, Boston University.

Other Sources

Alfonso X [el Sabio]. *Crónica general*. Edited by Marcelino Menéndez y Pelayo, 1:307–10. Madrid: Bailly-Balilliere e Hijos, 1906.

Alter, Robert. *Partial Magic: The Novel as a Self-conscious Genre*. Berkeley: University of California Press, 1975.

Aub, Max. *Discurso de la novela española contemporánea*. Mexico: Centro de Estudios Sociales, 1945.

Bakhtin, Mikhail. *Problems of Dostoevsky's Poetics*. Translated by R. W. Rotsel. Ann Arbor, Mich.: Ardis, 1973.

Barthes, Roland. *Writing Degree Zero*. Translated by Annette Lavers and Colin Smith. Boston: Beacon Press, 1970.

————. *Critical Essays*. Translated by Richard Howard. Evanston, Ill.: Northwestern University Press, 1972.

————. *S/Z*. Translated by Richard Miller. New York: Hill and Wang, 1974.

————. *The Pleasure of the Text*. Translated by Richard Miller. New York: Hill and Wang, 1975.

Benveniste, Emile. *Problems in General Linguistics*. Translated by Mary Meek. Coral Gables: University of Miami Press, 1971.

Bernstein, Jerome. "Body, Language, and Divinity in Goytisolo's *Juan sin tierra*." In *The Analysis of Hispanic Texts*. Edited by Lisa E. Davis and Isabel C. Terán. New York: Bilingual Press, 1976.

Bloom, Harold. *The Anxiety of Influence: A Theory of Poetry*. New York: Oxford University Press, 1973.

Borges, Jorge Luis. *Ficciones*. Buenos Aires: Emecé, 1956.

Buckley, Ramón. *Problemas formales de la novela española contemporánea*. Barcelona: Península, 1968.

Castro, Américo. *España en su historia*. Buenos Aires: Losada, 1948.

————. *La realidad histórica de España*. Mexico: Porrúa, 1954.

————. *Origen, ser y existir de los españoles*. Madrid: Taurus, 1959.

————. *The Spaniards: An Introduction to Their History*. Princeton, N.J.: Princeton University Press, 1972.

Cernuda, Luis. *Poesía completa*. Barcelona: Barral Editores, 1973.

Cervantes, Miguel de. *Don Quijote de la Mancha*. Edited by Martín de Riquer. Barcelona: Juventud, 1958.

Corrales Egea, José. *La novela española actual*. Madrid: Cuadernos para el Diálogo, 1971.

Couffon, Claude. "*Don Julián* ou la destruction des mythes." *Le Monde*, 11 September 1970, p. 10.

Culler, Jonathan. *Structuralist Poetics: Structuralism, Linguistics and the Study of Literature*. Ithaca, N.Y.: Cornell University Press, 1975.

Dällenbach, Lucien. "Intertexte et autotexte." *Poétique* 27 (1976): 282–96.

———. *Le récit spéculaire: Essai sur le mise en abyme*. Paris: Seuil, 1977.

De George, Richard T., and Fernande M. De George, eds. *The Structuralists: From Marx to Lévi-Strauss*. Garden City, N.Y.: Doubleday, 1972.

De Man, Paul. "The Rhetoric of Temporality." In *Interpretation: Theory and Practice*, edited by Charles S. Singleton, pp. 173–209. Baltimore: Johns Hopkins University Press, 1968.

Durán, Manuel. "Un orden desordenado: La estructura de *Juan sin tierra*." *Anales de la Novela de Posguerra* 3 (1978): 5–25.

Donato, Eugenio. "Structuralism: The Aftermath." *Sub-Stance* 7 (1973): 9–26.

Erlich, Victor. *Russian Formalism*. The Hague: Mouton, 1955.

Forrest, Gene Steven. "La destrucción del mito por medio del mito: Dos 'Prometeos' de la novela española." *Modern Language Notes* 93 (1978): 297–309.

Foucauld, Charles de. *Lettres à Mme de Bondy*. Paris: Desclée de Brouwer, 1966.

Frye, Northrop. *Anatomy of Criticism*. Princeton, N.J.: Princeton University Press, 1957.

Ganivet, Angel. *Idearium español y El porvenir de España*. Madrid: Espasa-Calpe, 1962.

García de Valdeavellano, Luis. *Historia de España*. Madrid: Revista de Occidente, 1968.

Gilman, Stephen. *The Spain of Fernando de Rojas*. Princeton, N.J.: Princeton University Press, 1972.

Gimferrer, Pere. "Riesgo y ventura de Juan Goytisolo." In *Juan Goytisolo: Obras completas*, 1:9–64. Madrid: Aguilar, 1977.

Goll, Ivan. *Jean sans terre*. Edited by Francis B. Carmody. University of California Publications in Modern Philology, no. 65. Berkeley: University of California Press, 1962.

Góngora, Luis de. *Obras completas*. Edited by Juan Millé y Giménez and Isabel Millé y Giménez. Madrid: Aguilar, 1961.

Guillén, Claudio. *Literature as System*. Princeton, N.J.: Princeton University Press, 1971.

Hernández, José. "Juan Goytisolo." *Modern Language Notes* 91 (1975): 337–55.

Herzberger, David. "The Theoretical Disparity of Contemporary Spanish Narrative." *Symposium* 33 (1979): 215–29.

Jameson, Fredric. *The Prison House of Language: A Critical Account of Structuralism and Russian Formalism.* Princeton, N.J.: Princeton University Press, 1972.

Kristeva, Julia. "Problèmes de la structuration de texte." In *Théorie d'ensemble,* pp. 298–317. Paris: Seuil, 1968.

———. *Le texte du roman: Approche sémiologique d'une structure discursive transformationelle.* The Hague: Mouton, 1970.

Larra, Mariano José de. *Artículos completos.* Edited by Melchor de Almagro. Madrid: Aguilar, 1968.

Lawrence, T. E. *Seven Pillars of Wisdom.* London: Jonathan Cape, 1973.

Lemon, Lee, and Marion J. Reis, eds. *Russian Formalist Criticism: Four Essays.* Lincoln: University of Nebraska Press, 1965.

Levine, Linda. "La aniquilación del catolicismo en *Reivindicación del Conde don Julián.*" *Norte* 13, nos. 4–6 (1972): 133–41.

———. *Juan Goytisolo: La destrucción creadora.* Mexico: Mortiz, 1976.

Levine, Susan F. " 'Cuerpo' y 'no cuerpo'—Una conjunción entre Juan Goytisolo y Octavio Paz." *Journal of Spanish Studies: Twentieth Century* 5 (1977): 123–35.

López-Morillas, Juan, ed. *Giner de los Ríos: Ensayos.* Madrid: Alianza Editorial, 1969.

Machado, Antonio. *Poesías completas.* Madrid: Espasa-Calpe, 1969.

Martínez Ruiz, José [Azorín]. *Obras selectas.* Madrid: Biblioteca Nueva, 1962.

Matejka, Ladislav, and Krystyna Pomorska, eds. and trans. *Readings in Russian Poetics: Formalist and Structuralist Views.* Cambridge, Mass.: MIT Press, 1971.

Menéndez Pidal, Ramón. *Reliquias de la poesía épica española.* Madrid: Espasa-Calpe, 1951.

Menéndez y Pelayo, Marcelino. *Historia de las ideas estéticas en España,* vol. 2. Madrid: Escritores Castellanos, 1889.

Navajas, Gonzalo U. *"Juan sin tierra:* Fin de un período novelístico." *Revista de Estudios Hispánicos* 13 (1979): 173–81.

———. *La novela de Juan Goytisolo.* Madrid: Sociedad General Española de Librería, 1979.

Ortega, José. *Juan Goytisolo: Alienación y agresión; "Señas de identidad" y "Reivindicación del Conde don Julián."* New York: Torres, 1972.

———. "Aproximación estructural a *Reivindicación del Conde don Julián.*" *Explicación de textos literarios* 3 (1974): 45–50.

Ortega, Julio. "An Interview with Juan Goytisolo." Translated by Joseph Schraibman. *Texas Quarterly* 18 (1975): 56–77.

Ortega y Gasset, José. *La caza y los toros.* Madrid: Espasa-Calpe, 1962.

Paz, Octavio. *Conjunciones y disyunciones.* Mexico: Mortiz, 1969.

———. *El mono gramático.* Barcelona: Seix Barral, 1974.

Pérez, Genaro. *Formalist Elements in the Novels of Juan Goytisolo.* Madrid: José Porrúa Turanzas, 1979.

Poirier, Richard. *The Performing Self: Compositions and Decompositions in the Languages of Contemporary Life.* New York: Oxford University Press, 1971.

Ramos, Alicia. "Unidad formal y análisis crítico de *Reivindicación del Conde don Julián.*" Ph.D. dissertation, Northwestern University, 1979.

Ríos, Fernando de los, ed. *El pensamiento de Giner de los Ríos.* Buenos Aires: Losada, 1949.

Ríos, Julián, ed. *Juan Goytisolo.* Madrid: Fundamentos, 1975.

———, ed. *Juan sin tierra.* Madrid: Fundamentos, 1977.

Robatto, Matilde. *La creación literaria de Juan Goytisolo.* Barcelona: Planeta, 1977.

Robbe-Grillet, Alain. *For a New Novel.* Translated by Richard Howard. New York: Grove Press, 1966.

Rodríguez Monegal, Emir. "Destrucción de la España sagrada." *Mundo Nuevo* 11 (1967): 46–60.

Romero, Héctor. "Los mitos de la España sagrada." *Journal of Spanish Studies: Twentieth Century* 1 (1973): 169–85.

Said, Edward W. *Beginnings: Intention and Method.* Baltimore: Johns Hopkins University Press, 1975.

Santullano, Luis, ed. *Romancero español.* Madrid: Aguilar, 1961.

Sarduy, Severo. "El barroco y el neo-barroco." In *América latina en su literatura,* edited by César Fernández Moreno, pp. 178–81. Mexico: Siglo Veintiuno, 1972.

———. *Escrito sobre un cuerpo.* Buenos Aires: Editorial Sudamericana, 1969.

Schwartz, Kessel. "Stylistic and Psychosexual Constants in the Novels of Juan Goytisolo." *Norte* 13, nos. 4–6 (1972): 119–28.

Sobejano, Gonzalo. "*Don Julián,* iconoclasta de la literatura patria." *Camp de l'arpa* 43–44 (1977): 7–14.

———. *Novela española de nuestro tiempo.* Madrid: Editorial Prensa Española, 1975.

Spires, Robert. "La autodestrucción creativa en *Reivindicación del Conde don Julián.*" *Journal of Spanish Studies: Twentieth Century* 4 (1976): 191–202.

———. "Latrines, Whirlpools, and Voids: The Metafictional Mode of *Juan sin tierra.*" *Hispanic Review* 48 (1980): 151–69.

———. "Modos narrativos y búsquedad de identidad en *Señas de identidad.*" *Anales de la Novela de Posguerra* 2 (1977): 55–72.

———. *La novela española de posguerra: Creación artística y experiencia social.* Madrid: Cupsa Editorial, 1978.

Todorov, Tzvetan. "Introduction." *Communications* 11 (1968): 1–4.

Trotsky, Leon. *Literature and Revolution.* New York: Russell and Russell, 1957.

Turmeda, Anselm. *Disputa de l'ase contra frare Encelm Turmeda sobre la natura y noblessa dels animals.* Translated by R. Foulché-Delbosc. "Disputacion de l'asne." *Revue Hispanique* 24 (1911): 358–479.

Ugarte, Michael. "Juan Goytisolo: Unruly Disciple of Américo Castro." *Journal of Spanish Studies: Twentieth Century* 7 (1979): 353–64.

———. "Juan Goytisolo's Mirrors: Intertextuality and Self-reflection in *Reivindicación del Conde don Julián* and *Juan sin tierra.*" *Modern Fiction Studies* 26 (1980–1981): 613–23.

Unamuno, Miguel de. *Obras completas,* vol. 1. Madrid: Escelicer, 1966.

Vegas González, Serafín. "La función terrorista del lenguaje." *Cuadernos Hispanoamericanos* 335 (1978): 190–212.

Wellek, René, and Austin Warren. *Theory of Literature.* New York: Harcourt, Brace and World, 1956.

Zamora Vicente, Alonso, ed. *Poema de Fernán González.* Madrid: Espasa-Calpe, 1946.

Index